The Cavaliers of the Confederacy: The Lives and Careers of JEB Stuart and Nathan Bedford Forrest

By Charles River Editors

About Charles River Editors

Charles River Editors was founded by Harvard and MIT alumni to provide superior editing and original writing services, with the expertise to create digital content for publishers across a vast range of subject matter. In addition to providing original digital content for third party publishers, Charles River Editors republishes civilization's greatest literary works, bringing them to a new generation via ebooks.

Visit charlesrivereditors.com for more information.

Introduction

James Ewell Brown Stuart (1833–1864)

"Calm, firm, acute, active, and enterprising, I know no one more competent than [Stuart] to estimate the occurrences before him at their true value." – General Joseph E. Johnston, 1861

Despite the fact that the Civil War was fought nearly 150 years ago, it remains a polarizing topic for the country to this day. But among the most popular perceptions of the Civil War is the "Lost Cause", which romanticized the war's toughest and most famous fighters and continues to fuel the popularity of generals like Robert E. Lee.

Alongside Lee, no one epitomized the chivalry and heroism celebrated by the Lost Cause more than JEB Stuart (1833-1864), the most famous cavalry officer of the Civil War. Stuart was equal parts great and grandiose, leading the cavalry for the Confederacy in Lee's Army of Northern Virginia until his death at the Battle of Yellow Tavern in May 1864. Stuart was a throwback to the past, colorfully dressing with capes, sashes, and an ostrich plumed hat, while sporting cologne and a heavy beard. But he was also brilliant in conducting reconnaissance, and he proved capable of leading both cavalry and infantry at battles like Chancellorsville. As the eyes and ears of Robert E. Lee's army, none were better, despite the fact that he was only in his late 20s and early 30s during the Civil War, far younger than most men of senior rank.

Nevertheless, Stuart's tough fighting was and still is eclipsed by his reputation for audacious cavalry movements. He embarrassed the Army of the Potomac by riding around it twice, making him famous and embarrassing Union generals like George McClellan. However, Stuart's role at Gettysburg was far more controversial. Given great discretion in his cavalry operations before the battle, Stuart's cavalry was too far removed from the Army of Northern Virginia to warn Lee of the Army of the Potomac's movements. Lee's army inadvertently stumbled into the Union army at Gettysburg, walking blindly into what became the largest battle of the war. Stuart has been heavily criticized ever since, and it is said Lee took him to task when he arrived on the second day, leading Stuart to offer his resignation. Lee didn't accept it, but he would later note in his after battle report that the cavalry had not updated him as to the Army of the Potomac's movements.

With his record and characteristics, it has proven almost impossible for Americans to hold a neutral view of Stuart, and it has been even harder to ignore him. *The Cavaliers of the Confederacy* addresses the controversies and battles that made Stuart famous, but it also humanizes the man who was courageous and cocky, yet self-conscious enough to hide what he considered to be a weak chin. Along with pictures of Stuart and other important people, places and events in his life, you will learn about the Confederacy's most famous cavalier like you never have before, in no time at all.

Nathan Bedford Forrest (1821–1877)

"I got there first with the most men." – Nathan Bedford Forrest

Despite the fact that the Civil War was fought nearly 150 years ago, it remains a polarizing topic for the country to this day. And nowhere is this more evident than in the life and legacy of Confederate Lieutenant General Nathan Bedford Forrest, the war's most controversial soldier.

When the war broke out, Forrest enlisted in the army and was instructed to raise a battalion of cavalry. A self-made man with no formal military training, Forrest spent the entire war fighting in the Western theater, becoming the only individual in the war to rise from the rank of Private to Lieutenant General. By the end of the war, Forrest was known throughout the South as the "Wizard of the Saddle," and anecdotes of his prowess in battle were legendary. In addition to being injured multiple times in battle, Forrest has been credited with having killed 30 Union soldiers in combat and having 29 horses shot out from under him.

History has properly accorded Forrest his place as one of the most courageous soldiers of the Civil War, and Forrest attained a number of command successes in the Western theater of the war. But Forrest was also at the head of Confederate troops accused of massacring a Union garrison comprised mostly of black soldiers at Fort Pillow, and he was also a prominent slave trader, an overt racist, and likely a leader of the Ku Klux Klan after the Civil War. When he died in 1877, in part due to various war wounds, he was the nation's most notorious unreconstructed rebel. John E. Stanchack, an editor of the *Civil War Times Illustrated*, aptly noted in 1993, "Everything…about [Forrest] is bent to fit some political or intellectual agenda." Ashdown and Caudill, authors of *The Myth of Nathan Bedford Forrest*, write that the story of Forrest "embraces violence, race, realism, sectionalism, politics, reconciliation, and repentance."

With these characteristics, it has proven almost impossible for any American to have a neutral view of Forrest, and it has been even harder to ignore him. Subsequently, Forrest's image has vacillated from celebrated to reviled, sometimes both at the same time, over the last 150 years, as the numerous and notable aspects of Forrest's life and legacy were considered by different people at different times. *The Cavaliers of the Confederacy* addresses the controversies and battles within Forrest's war record, but it also humanizes the man, explaining what drove him before and after the war. Along with pictures of Forrest and other important people, places and events in his life, you will learn about the Wizard of the Saddle like you never have before, in no time at all.

JEB Stuart

Chapter 1: Childhood and Early Years, 1833-1854

The Stuart Family Tree

Young Stuart before the beard

JEB Stuart has long been viewed as one of the Confederacy's bravest soldiers, and a symbol of the perfect Christian, Virginian soldier that defeated Rebels turned to after the war. Stuart's destiny and legacy, of course, always centered around the Old Dominion.

James Ewell Brown "Jeb/J. E. B." Stuart was born at Laurel Hill plantation in Patrick County, Virginia, near the North Carolina border on February 6, 1833, the eighth of 11 children to Archibald Stuart and Elizabeth Letcher Pannill. His family ancestry in America began with Archibald and brother David Stuart who sought refuge from religious persecution (presumably in Ireland) by emigrating to Chester County, Pennsylvania in 1726, and subsequently moving again with his family (which included Judge John Stuart of Londonderry, Ireland) to Augusta County, Virginia about 1738.

Like Robert E. Lee, the superior he will always be associated with, Stuart was imbued with a sense of dignity and responsibility that was based in no small part on his family's military and political service. The first generation of American-born Stuarts was distinguished by the military services of Major Alexander Stuart (James' great grandfather), who nearly died of wounds sustained at the Battle of Guilford Court House during the American Revolution. Alexander's son, John, lived for a time in the West serving as a Federal judge in Illinois and Missouri, and as Speaker of the House of Representatives in Missouri.

John's son, Archibald was a veteran of the War of 1812, a slaveholder, an attorney, and a Democrat who represented Patrick County in both Houses of the Virginia General Assembly. Archibald married Elizabeth Pannill, who herself was a descendant of the prominent Letcher family, and together produced 11 children, Jeb being their eighth. Elizabeth was known as a strict, religious woman, and in an unusual role for the time period, she essentially ran the family plantation.

The Shaping of a Leader

In 1959, author Gertrude Hecker Winders published what was for many years considered a fair depiction of the boyhood life of "Jeb" Stuart, *Jeb Stuart: Boy in the Saddle*. In recent years, however, as part of an ongoing reexamination of Stuart's life, many critics and historians now believe it more a fanciful account based on urban legend, generalities, and supposition. While that was fittingly in keeping with the reputation and legacy Stuart would carve during the Civil War, the color of the stories has since been called heavily into question.

As a result, it seems that little verifiable information concerning Stuart's early life was written in his time, or it has yet to be uncovered. There are, however, a few well-documented events that can offer insight into the man who came to be known primarily by his various high-profile exploits during the Civil War.

Jeb was the youngest of the five sons who lived beyond childhood, and his father, Archibald, was a prominent politician and attorney who represented Patrick County in both Houses of the Virginia General Assembly and served one term in the U. S. House of Representatives. Jeb's mother, Elizabeth, was known as a stern, religious woman with a great love of nature who ran the family plantation. There can be little doubt that like most boys in this place and time in American history, young Jeb had his share of chores and responsibilities, and received a basic education as time permitted. By surviving accounts, Jeb enjoyed a "happy boyhood," loved his family home at Laurel Hill, displayed an enthusiasm for nature, and often said that one of his fondest dreams for adulthood was to one day own his family home and end his days there in quiet retirement.

The Stuart home has been described as "an unpretentious, comfortable farmhouse" which, tragically, was destroyed by fire in the winter of 1847-48, though no detailed description of the house remains. In a surviving letter, Jeb described the fire as "a sad disaster."

For a few years after the fire, Archibald and son John Dabney lived in the outbuilding that had served as the family kitchen; with Archibald apparently remaining there until his death in 1855. In 1859, Elizabeth Stuart sold the property to two men from Mt. Airy, North Carolina, and the Laurel Hill plantation passed out of the Stuart family's possession.

Although few personal anecdotes regarding the young Jeb survive, one incident that seems to foretell of the bravery and audacity he would later display as a Civil War officer occurred at about the age of ten. As the story is told, while walking through the woods one afternoon with an older brother, a swarm of hornets attacked the two, sending the elder brother running. Young Jeb, however, is said to have "narrowed his eyes defiantly" and knocked the hornets' nest to the ground with a stick, defying the danger the bees posed. As would be seen repeatedly on the battlefield, James seems to have thrived on danger from a very early age.

Formal Education

Jeb received his earliest education at home, lessons presented by his mother and various relatives and neighbors, until 1845, when at the age of 12 he left Laurel Hill to be educated by a series of teachers in Wytheville, Virginia, and at the home of his aunt Anne (Archibald's sister) and her husband Judge James Ewell Brown (Stuart's namesake) at Danville. During the summer of 1848, Jeb became fascinated with military life and attempted to enlist in the U. S. Army, but the 15 year old teenager was rejected due to his age. That fall he entered Emory & Henry College, a private liberal arts school in Emory, Virginia where he studied for the next two years.

Finally, in 1850, Jeb gained entry into the military life he sought, appointed to the United States Military Academy at West Point, New York, by family friend, Representative Thomas Hamlet Averett, a man who had defeated James' father in the 1848 House election.

West Point, 1850-1854

In 1850, Jeb entered the U. S. Military Academy at West Point and quickly adapted to military rigors, becoming a popular, happy student. Though not considered handsome during his teen years, and standing just five foot, nine inches tall, James' classmates began calling him "Beauty," which they explained as his "personal comeliness in inverse ratio to the term employed."[1] He is said to have possessed a chin "so short and retiring as positively to disfigure his otherwise fine countenance." The weak chin did not escape his notice, and after graduation he would grow a beard that led a fellow officer to remark, "[He was] the only man I ever saw that [a] beard improved."[2]

---

[1]   Thomas, Emory M. *Bold Dragoon: The Life of J.E.B. Stuart.* Page 18.

[2]   Davis, Burke. *Jeb Stuart: The Last Cavalier.* Page 33.

Today West Point is the country's elite military academy, but when Stuart entered the school in 1850, its importance in training the Civil War's greatest leaders was not yet known, and the campus hardly befitted a great institution. In 1852, Robert E. Lee, who had a legendary reputation at the Academy for finishing first in his class and not receiving a demerit nearly 20 years earlier, was appointed superintendent of the Academy, and Jeb soon became friends with the Lee family, seeing them socially on numerous occasions. Lee's nephew, Fitzhugh Lee (who would serve under Jeb during the Civil War as a lieutenant colonel of the First Virginia Cavalry beginning in August 1861), also arrived at the academy that year.

It was at West Point that Stuart proved to himself and others his cavalry talents. In his final year at West Point, in addition to achieving the cadet rank of second captain of the corps, he was one of only eight cadets designated "honorary cavalry officers" for his exceptional skills in horsemanship. In 1854, at the age of 21, Jeb graduated thirteenth in his class of forty-six, ranked tenth in his class in cavalry tactics. And although he enjoyed the civil engineering curriculum and did well in mathematics as well, his poor drawing skills hampered his engineering studies, so he finished 29th in that discipline. (A Stuart family legend insists that he deliberately slacked-off his academic studies his final year to avoid service in the elite--but dull--Army Corps of Engineers.)

In October of 1854, James was commissioned brevet Second Lieutenant James Ewell Brown Stuart, but he was already most often referred to as "Jeb." Of course, Stuart would be remembered as one of a handful of West Point men who became the greatest generals of the Civil War, and the future generals' years at West Point became a source of colorful stories about the men who would become Civil War legends. In 1846, a shy kid named Thomas Jonathan Jackson made few friends and struggled with his studies, finishing 17th in his class 15 years before becoming Stonewall, while George Pickett was more preoccupied with playing hooky at a local bar before finishing last in the same class as Jackson. A.P. Hill was already in love with the future wife of George McClellan, a young prodigy who finished second in his class, while a clerical error by West Point administrators ensured that Hiram Ulysses Grant forever became known as Ulysses S. Grant. And years after Robert E. Lee met Albert Sidney Johnston and Jefferson Davis at West Point, William Tecumseh Sherman was roommates with George H. Thomas, who later became one of his principal subordinates and the "Rock of Chickamauga".

Lee

Chapter 2: Early Military Service, 1855-1861

Forts Davis and Leavenworth

On January 28, 1855, brevet Second Lieutenant James "Jeb" Stuart was assigned to the U. S. Mounted Rifles Cavalry at Fort Davis, Texas (in what is today Jeff Davis County), becoming a leader on scouting missions over the San Antonio to El Paso Road, where for the next three months he fought the Apaches. He was then transferred to the newly formed First Cavalry Regiment at Fort Leavenworth, Kansas Territory, where he became regimental quartermaster and commissary officer under the command of Colonel Edwin V. Sumner. His organizational and logistical talents quickly becoming apparent, he was promoted to first lieutenant later that same year.

Edwin "Bull" Sumner would lead a corps for the Army of the Potomac in the major campaigns of 1862

Bleeding Kansas

In an attempt to organize the center of North America – Kansas and Nebraska – without offsetting the slave-free balance, Senator Stephen Douglas of Illinois proposed the Kansas-Nebraska Act. The Kansas-Nebraska Act eliminated the Missouri Compromise line of 1820, which the Compromise of 1850 had maintained. The Missouri Compromise had stipulated that states north of the boundary line determined in that bill would be free, and that states south of it *could* have slavery. This was essential to maintaining the balance of slave and free states in the Union. The Kansas-Nebraska Act, however, ignored the line completely and proposed that all new territories be organized by popular sovereignty. Settlers could vote whether they wanted their state to be slave or free.

When popular sovereignty became the standard in Kansas and Nebraska, the primary result was that thousands of zealous pro-slavery and anti-slavery advocates both moved to Kansas to influence the vote, creating a dangerous (and ultimately deadly) mix. Numerous attacks took place between the two sides, and many pro-slavery Missourians organized attacks on Kansas towns just across the border.

The best known abolitionist in Bleeding Kansas was a middle aged man named John Brown. A radical abolitionist, Brown organized a small band of like-minded followers and fought with the armed groups of pro-slavery men in Kansas for several months, including a notorious incident known as the Pottawatomie Massacre, in which Brown's supporters murdered five men. Over 56 people died until John Brown left the territory, which ultimately entered the Union as a free state in 1859.

John Brown

Now a veteran of the Native American frontier conflicts, from 1855 to 1861 First Lieutenant Stuart was given a leadership position in defusing "Bleeding Kansas" (or the "Border War"), the violent political confrontations between anti-slavery "Free-Staters" (like John Brown) and pro-slavery "Border Ruffians" that took place in the Kansas Territory and neighboring towns of Missouri, and ended with the "Pottawatomie Massacre."

Battle of Solomon's River

On July 29, 1857, Stuart demonstrated his knack for initiative and bravery during the Cheyenne uprising known as the Battle of Solomon's River in present day Kansas. According to reports, after his commander, Colonel Sumner, ordered a "drawn sabers" charge against a band of Cheyenne who were firing a barrage of arrows, Stuart and three other lieutenants chased one Cheyenne down, who Stuart then shot in the thigh. The Native American, however, turned and fired at Stuart with a flintlock, striking him directly in the chest, but doing little actual damage. By the time Stuart returned to Fort Leavenworth that September to reunite with his family, word of his courage and exceptional leadership abilities preceded him.

Harpers Ferry

After his activities in Kansas, Brown spent the next few years raising money in New England, which would bring him into direct contact with important abolitionist leaders, including Frederick Douglass. Brown had previously organized a small raiding party that succeeded in raiding a Missouri farm and freeing 11 slaves, but he set his sights on far larger objectives. In 1859, Brown began to set a new plan in motion that he hoped would create a full scale slave uprising in the South. Brown's plan relied on raiding Harpers Ferry, a strategically located armory in western Virginia that had been the main federal arms depot after the Revolution. Given its proximity to the South, Brown hoped to seize thousands of rifles and move them south, gathering slaves and swelling his numbers as he went. The slaves would then be armed and ready to help free more slaves, inevitably fighting Southern militias along the way.

In recognition of how important Douglass had become among abolitionists, Brown attempted to enlist the support of Douglass by informing him of the plans. While Douglass didn't blow the whistle on Brown, he told Brown that violence would only further enrage the South, and slaveholders might only retaliate further against slaves with devastating consequences. Instead of helping Brown, Douglass dissuaded freed blacks from joining Brown's group because he believed it was doomed to fail.

In July 1859, Brown traveled to Harper's Ferry under an assumed name and waited for his recruits, but he struggled to get even 20 people to join him. Rather than call off the plan, however, Brown went ahead with it. That fall, Brown and his men used hundreds of rifles to seize the armory at Harper's Ferry, but the plan went haywire from the start, and word of his attack quickly spread. Local pro-slavery men formed a militia and pinned Brown and his men down while they were still at the armory. With Robert E. Lee commanding the marines surrounding Brown, some of Brown's men were killed and Brown was captured.

Young Jeb Stuart played an active role in opposing the raid at Harpers Ferry. In October of 1859, while conducting business in Washington, D.C., Stuart volunteered to carry secret instructions to Lieutenant Colonel Robert E. Lee and then accompany him and a squad of U. S. Military Militia to Harpers Ferry, where Brown had staged a raid on the armory. While delivering Lee's written ultimatum to the leader of the raid, who was going by the pseudonym Isaac Smith, Stuart remembered "Old Ossawatomie Brown" from the events at Bleeding Kansas, and ultimately assisted in his arrest.

The fallout from John Brown's raid on Harpers Ferry was intense. Southerners had long suspected that abolitionists hoped to arm the slaves and use violence to abolish slavery, and Brown's raid seemed to confirm that. Meanwhile, much of the northern press praised Brown for his actions. In the South, conspiracy theories ran wild about who had supported the raid, and many believed prominent abolitionist Republicans had been behind the raid as well. On the day of his execution, Brown wrote, "I, John Brown, am now quite *certain* that the crimes of this *guilty land* will never be purged away but with *blood.* I had, as I now think vainly, flattered myself that without very much bloodshed it might be done."

On April 22, 1861, First Lieutenant Stuart received a commission as captain in the U. S. Army, but this came 10 days after the assault on Fort Sumter, recognized as the beginning of the Civil War. After Abraham Lincoln's election in 1860, a handful of Southern states had already seceded, and Virginia would join them after Sumter. By the time Stuart received the promotion, he was already determined to fight with Virginia, and thus the Confederacy, in the civil conflict.

A little over a week later, in early May, he tendered his resignation from the Federal army.

Chapter 3: Personal Life, 1855 to 1864

Marriage

In July of 1855 while stationed at Fort Leavenworth, Kansas Territory, Stuart met Flora Cooke, daughter of Lieutenant Colonel Philip St. George Cooke, commander of the Second U. S. Dragoon Regiment. (Cooke is noted for his authorship of the standard Army Cavalry Manual and is sometimes called the "Father of the U. S. Cavalry.") Biographer and historian Burke Davis described Flora as "an accomplished horsewoman, and though not pretty, an effective charmer," to whom "Stuart succumbed with hardly a struggle."[3]

In September of that year, less than two months after meeting, Stuart proposed marriage. In a clever play off another famous general's words, Stuart wrote of his whirlwind courtship, "*Veni, Vidi, Victus sum,*" Latin for "I came, I saw, I was conquered".[4] Although the couple had planned a gala wedding at Fort Riley, Kansas, the death of Stuart's father on September 20, 1855, brought a change of plans, with the wedding subsequently held on November 14, attended only by family members.

In 1856 the couple's first child, a girl, was born, but died the same day. Then on November 14, 1857, Flora gave birth to a second daughter whom they named Flora. In early 1858 the Stuart's relocated to Fort Riley, Kansas with their two slaves--one inherited from his father's estate, one purchased to help around the Stuart household--where they remained until 1859.

In October of 1859, while still in service to the U. S. Army, Stuart developed a new saber hook, "an improved method of attaching sabers to belts"--for which the U. S. government paid him $5,000 for a "right to use" license. It was while he was in Washington discussing the contract (and applying for an appointment to the quartermaster department) that Stuart heard about John Brown's raid on the U. S. Arsenal at Harpers Ferry and volunteered to be Colonel Lee's *aide-de-camp*.

On June 26, 1860, wife Flora gave birth to a son who would at first be named Philip St. George Cooke Stuart, after Jeb's well known father in law.

---

3   Davis, Burke. *Jeb Stuart: The Last Cavalier.* Page 36.

4   Wert, Jeffry D. *Cavalryman of the Lost Cause: A Biography of J.E.B. Stuart.* Pages 30--31.

The War Years

On April 22, 1861, Stuart was promoted to captain of the U. S. Army, but following the secession of Virginia, on May 3, 1861, resigned his commission to join the Army of the Confederate States.

Moving his family to Virginia, on May 10, 1861, "Jeb" was commissioned a lieutenant colonel of the Virginia Infantry. Meanwhile, his father-in-law, Philip St. George Cooke, chose not to resign his Army commission, prompting Stuart to write his wife that it would "do irreparable injury to our only son" to have him named after Cooke. "Jeb" wrote to his brother-in-law (future Confederate Brig. General John Rogers Cooke) saying, "[Philip] will regret it but once, and that will be continuously."[5] After consideration, "Jeb" and Flora renamed the boy, James Ewell Brown Stuart, Jr., an obvious indicator of his disgust with his father-in-law's political views.

Colonel Cooke

Once Jeb left for Richmond to join the fighting, Flora settled in at Wytheville, Virginia, arranging to sometimes stay at or near her husband's camp where they could share meals, music, and conversation. Even so, their frequent separations strained their relationship, and it didn't help that in addition to writing frequently to his wife, "Jeb" also carried on correspondences with other women attracted to his fame. Although the couple acknowledged these exchanges as "insubstantial flirtations," Flora detested the photographs and gifts the women sent, and wrote of feeling laughed at for her husband's fondness for society and the ladies. But by all other accounts, "Jeb" was a thoughtful and romantic husband who always carried his wife's photograph in a silver frame near his heart.

---

[5]   Wright, C. M. "Flora Cooke Stuart (1836–1923)."

On November 3, 1862, while "Jeb" was with the Army of Northern Virginia during the early stages of what would become the Fredericksburg campaign, their daughter Flora died of typhoid fever. In the following weeks, Stuart wrote that his wife was "not herself since the loss of her little companion." The following October, their daughter Virginia Pelham was born--both easing the pain and intensifying the loss. Flora wrote, "She is said to be like Little Flora. I hope she is."[6]

Chapter 4: 1861

The Start of the War

Despite having virtually zero support in the slave states, Abraham Lincoln ascended to the presidency at the head of a party that was not yet 10 years old, and one whose stated goal was to end the expansion of slavery. Although Lincoln did not vow to abolish slavery altogether, southerners believed Lincoln's presidency constituted a direct threat to the South's economy and political power, both of which were fueled by the slave system. Southerners also perceived the end of the expansion of slavery as a threat to their constitutional rights, and the rights of their states, frequently invoking northern states' refusals to abide by the Fugitive Slave Act.

Lincoln's predecessor was among those who could see the potential conflict coming from a mile away. While still in office, President James Buchanan instructed the federal army to permit the Confederacy to take control of forts in its territory, hoping to avoid a war. Conveniently, this also allowed Southern forces to take control of important forts and land ahead of a potential war, which would make secession and/or a victory in a military conflict easier. Many Southern partisans in federal government in 1860 took advantage of these opportunities to help Southern states ahead of time.

One of the forts in the South was Fort Sumter, an important but undermanned and undersupplied fort in the harbor of Charleston, South Carolina. Buchanan attempted to resupply Fort Sumter in the first few months of 1860, but the attempt failed when Southern sympathizers in the harbor fired on the resupply ship.

In his First Inaugural Address, Lincoln promised that it would not be the North that started a potential war, but he was also aware of the possibility of the South initiating conflict. After he was sworn in, Lincoln sent word to the Governor of South Carolina that he was sending ships to resupply Fort Sumter, to which the governor replied demanding that federal forces evacuate it. Southern forces again fired on the ship sent to resupply the boat, and on April 12, 1861,

---

6   Thomas, Emory M. *Bold Dragoon: The Life of J.E.B. Stuart*. Page 95.

Confederate artillery began bombarding Fort Sumter itself. After nearly 36 hours of bombardment, Major Robert Anderson called for a truce with Southern forces led by P.G.T. Beauregard, and the fort was officially surrendered on April 14. No casualties were caused on either side by the dueling bombardments across the harbor, but, ironically, two Union soldiers were killed by an accidental explosion during the surrender ceremonies.

After the attack on Fort Sumter, support for both the northern and southern cause rose. President Lincoln requested that each loyal state raise regiments for the defense of the Union, with the intent of raising an enormous army that would subdue the rebellion. However, four states which had been avoiding seceding or declaring support for the Union seceded after Lincoln's call for volunteers. The Confederate States of America now consisted of South Carolina, Mississippi, Florida, Alabama, Georgia, Louisiana, Texas, Virginia, Arkansas, North Carolina and Tennessee. The border states of Kentucky, Maryland, and Delaware remained in the Union, but the large number of southern sympathizers in these states buoyed the Confederates' hopes that those too would soon join the South.

Despite the loss of Fort Sumter, the North expected a relatively quick victory. Their expectations weren't unrealistic, due to the Union's overwhelming economic advantages over the South. At the start of the war, the Union had a population of over 22 million. The South had a population of 9 million, nearly 4 million of whom were slaves. Union states contained 90% of the manufacturing capacity of the country and 97% of the weapon manufacturing capacity. Union states also possessed over 70% of the total railroads in the pre-war United States at the start of the war, and the Union also controlled 80% of the shipbuilding capacity of the pre-war United States.

The firing on Fort Sumter and Lincoln's call to arms brought events quickly to a head. Now Virginia, which had delayed commitment as long as possible, had to choose sides, and with its secession in April 1861, Stuart joined the Confederacy.

Lieutenant Colonel Stuart

On May 10, 1861, Stuart was commissioned a lieutenant colonel of the Virginia Infantry and ordered by Maj. General Robert E. Lee to report to Colonel Thomas J. Jackson at Harpers Ferry. Stuart's reputation had clearly made the rounds, because when he reported to the man who would months later become Stonewall Jackson, Jackson ignored Stuart's infantry designation and instead assigned him command of all the cavalry companies of the Army of the Shenandoah, organized as the First Virginia Cavalry Regiment. Thus, on July 4, 1861, Jeb Stuart began his service in the Confederate cavalry, less than 3 weeks before the First Battle of Bull Run.

Stonewall Jackson

Although Stuart would soon appear in his trademark flamboyant line attire--a scarlet-lined gray cape, yellow sash, hat cocked to the side displaying a peacock plume, jack boots, gauntlets, red flower in his lapel, and full red beard doused with cologne (reminiscent of commanders of the Napoleonic era)--when he accepted his Confederate commission, he was still wearing his Federal uniform and would do so even as he fought at Falling Waters, Virginia, on July 2, 1861. And while most Confederate officers were somehow distinguishable on the battlefield, Stuart--whose horse "Highfly" soon became as famous as his extraordinary rider--became one of the most visually stunning.

Quickly becoming one of the most dominant commanders in the field, on July 16, Stuart was promoted to Full Colonel of the First Virginia Cavalry.

First Battle of Bull Run or Manassas

After Fort Sumter, the Lincoln Administration pushed for a quick invasion of Virginia, with the intent of defeating Confederate forces and marching toward the Confederate capitol of Richmond. Lincoln pressed Irvin McDowell to push forward. Despite the fact that McDowell knew his troops were inexperienced and unready, pressure from the Washington politicians forced him to launch a premature offensive against Confederate forces in northern Virginia.

McDowell's strategy during the First Battle of Bull Run was grand, and in many ways it was the forerunner of a tactic Lee and Jackson executed brilliantly on nearly the same field during the Second Battle of Bull Run or Manassas in August 1862. McDowell's plan called for parts of his army to pin down P.G.T. Beauregard's Confederate soldiers in front while marching another wing of his army around the flank and into the enemy's rear, rolling up the line. McDowell assumed the Confederates, led by General P. G. T. Beauregard, would be forced to abandon Manassas Junction and fall back to the next defensible line, the Rappahannock River. In July 1861, however, this proved far too difficult for his inexperienced troops to carry out effectively.

The First Battle of Bull Run made history in several ways. McDowell's army met Fort Sumter hero P.G.T. Beauregard's Confederate army near the railroad junction at Manassas on July 21, 1861. Located just 25 miles away from Washington D.C., many civilians from Washington came to watch what they expected to be a rout of Confederate forces. And for awhile, it appeared as though that might be the case.

McDowell's strategy fell apart though, thanks to railroads. Confederate reinforcements under General Joseph E. Johnston's Army, including Stuart's cavalrymen and a brigade led by Jackson, arrived by train in the middle of the day, a first in the history of American warfare. With Johnston's army arriving midday on July 21, it evened up the numbers between Union and Confederate. Shoring up the Confederates' left flank, some of Johnston's troops led by Jackson helped reverse the Union's momentum and ultimately turn the tide. As the battle's momentum switched, the inexperienced Union troops were routed and retreated in disorder back toward Washington in an unorganized mass. With over 350 killed on each side, it was the deadliest battle in American history to date, and both the Confederacy and the Union were quickly served notice that the war would be much more costly than either side had believed.

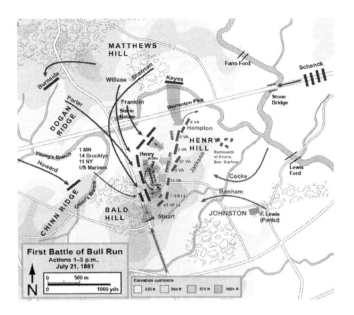

First Battle of Bull Run
Actions 1–3 p.m.,
July 21, 1861

Ironically, McDowell commanded the Army of Northeastern Virginia and Joseph E. Johnston commanded the Army of the Potomac at First Bull Run. A little over a year later it would be Lee's Army of Northern Virginia fighting elements of the Union Army of the Potomac at Second Bull Run, on nearly the same ground.

It was also during First Manassas or Bull Run that Jackson earned the famous nickname "Stonewall", but there is an enduring mystery over the origin of his nickname. What is known is that during the battle, Jackson's brigade arrived as reinforcements at a crucial part of the battlefield on the Confederate left. Confederate Brigadier General Barnard Bee, commanding a nearby brigade, commanded his men to reestablish their battle line next to Jackson's brigade, shouting, "There is Jackson standing like a stone wall. Rally behind the Virginians."

General Bee was mortally wounded shortly after that command and died the following day. Thus, it remains unclear whether Bee was complimenting Jackson's brigade for standing firm or whether he was criticizing Jackson's brigade for inaction. Without Bee around to explain his command, nobody will ever know for certain. However, that has not stopped people from debating Bee's comment.

While Bee's comment might be interpreted as inaction, Jackson was badly wounded in the thick of the battle, ironically because he insisted on raising his arm during the battle, apparently as a result of his "unbalanced body" quirk. While doing that, his arm was hit by a bullet. Regardless, the nickname Stonewall stuck, and Jackson was henceforth known as Stonewall Jackson. His brigade also inherited the title, known throughout the war as the Stonewall brigade.

General Bee

Jackson eventually emerged as the man who gained the most fame during the battle, but others at the time thought the man of the hour was Jeb Stuart. When Jackson's brigade turned the tide, Stuart then executed a highly-aggressive charge during which, "[the] Confederate cavalry-men were armed with costly English shot guns, which they held at the breast and fired (both barrels at once) as they approached . . . ."[7] In a panic, many of McDowell's men ran frantically toward Washington, with Stuart's cavalry among the units pursuing them some 12 miles, and subsequently taking the Union headquarters on Munson's hill (within sight of Washington). Of this remarkable Confederate victory, General Jubal Early, who served under Stonewall Jackson, wrote: "Stuart did as much toward saving the Battle of First Manassas as any subordinate who participated in it."[8]

From this point on, Stuart's celebrity grew, and he became known as Stuart "the brash," Stuart "the fearless," Stuart the "*beau sabreur* of mounted infantry." By war's end, however, critics would label him Stuart "the impetuous," and Stuart the "egotistical."

---

[7]   Stepp, John W. & Hill, William I. (editors), *Mirror of War, the Washington Star Reports the Civil War*. Page 145.
[8]   Sifakis, Stewart, "Who Was Who In The Civil War."

Brigadier General Stuart

After commanding the Confederate Army's outposts along the upper Potomac River at Fairfax Court House and Munson's Hill, Stuart was then given command of the cavalry of the ironically named Army of the Potomac, which eventually became the Army of Northern Virginia. On September 24, 1861, Stuart was promoted to Brigadier General. Among those advocating his promotion was General Joseph E. Johnston who in August wrote to Confederate President Jefferson Davis saying: "[Stuart] is a rare man, wonderfully endowed by nature with the qualities necessary for an officer of light cavalry. Calm, firm, acute, active, and enterprising, I know no one more competent than he to estimate the occurrences before him at their true value. If you add to this army a real brigade of cavalry, you can find no better brigadier-general to command it."[9]

Chapter 5: 1862

Stuart's Most Famous Ride: The Peninsula Campaign of 1862

During the Civil War, one of the tales that was often told among Confederate soldiers was that Joseph E. Johnston was a crack shot who was a better bird hunter than just about everyone else in the South. However, as the story went, Johnston would never take the shot when asked to, complaining that something was wrong with the situation that prevented him from being able to shoot the bird when it was time. The story is almost certainly apocryphal, used to demonstrate the Confederates' frustration with a man who everyone regarded as a capable general. Johnston began the Civil War as one of the senior commanders, leading (ironically) the Army of the Potomac to victory in the Battle of First Bull Run over Irvin McDowell's Union Army. But Johnston would become known more for losing by not winning. Johnston was never badly beaten in battle, but he had a habit of "strategically withdrawing" until he had nowhere else to go.

---

[9]   Wert, Jeffry D. *Cavalryman of the Lost Cause: A Biography of J.E.B. Stuart.* Page 62.

General Johnston

Despite Union successes in the Western theater, the focus of the Lincoln Administration remained concentrated on Richmond. The loss at Bull Run prompted a changing of the guard, with George McClellan, the "Young Napoleon", put in charge of reorganizing and leading the Army of the Potomac. McClellan had finished second in his class at West Point and was a well-regarded engineer, not to mention a foreign observer at the siege of Sevastopol during the Crimean War. This experience made him fit for commanding an army, but it also colored his military ideology in a way that was at odds with a Lincoln Administration that was eager for aggressive action and movement toward Richmond.

Under McClellan, and at Lincoln's urging, the Army of the Potomac conducted an ambitious amphibious invasion of Virginia in the spring of 1862. McClellan hoped to circumvent Confederate defenses to the north of Richmond by attacking Richmond from the southeast, landing his giant army on the Virginian peninsula. McClellan originally surprised the Confederates with his movement, but the narrow peninsula made it easier for Confederate forces to defend. One heavily outnumbered force led by John Magruder famously held out under siege at Yorktown for nearly an entire month, slowing the Army of the Potomac down. Magruder used a tactic of marching his men up and down the siege lines repeatedly to give the appearance he had several times more men than he actually had.

General Magruder

Lee advised Davis to consider a compromise that would protect Richmond from the North and keep Union generals McDowell and McClellan from joining forces. While Johnston's army would stay between McClellan and Richmond, Lee suggested that General "Stonewall" Jackson be ordered to muster all his units and drive toward the Potomac, striking heavily at whatever stood in his path. Jackson would go on to lead an army to one of the most incredible campaigns of the war in the Shenandoah Valley in 1862. Known as the Valley Campaign, Jackson kept 3 Union armies occupied north of Richmond with less than 1/3 of the men. Jackson's forces marched about 650 miles in just 3 months, earning the nickname "foot cavalry."

Throughout May 1862, Stuart's cavalry screened Johnston's army and defended as rear guard when Johnston's army retreated ever closer back to Richmond. Johnston continued his strategic retreats toward Richmond until McClellan's Army of the Potomac got close enough to Richmond that they could see the city's church steeples. But after word of General Jackson's startling victories over McDowell and his subsequent retreat were received, Johnston learned that McClellan was moving along the Chickahominy River. It was at this point that Johnston got uncharacteristically aggressive.

Johnston had run out of breathing space for his army, and he believed McClellan was seeking to link up with McDowell's forces. Therefore he drew up a very complex plan of attack for different wings of his army, and struck at the Army of the Potomac at the Battle of Seven Pines on May 31, 1862. Like McDowell's plan for First Bull Run, the plan proved too complicated for

Johnston's army to execute, and after a day of bloody fighting little was accomplished from a technical standpoint. However, McClellan was rattled by the attack, and Johnston was seriously wounded during the fighting, resulting in Lee being sent to assume command of the Army of Northern Virginia.

From his first day in command, Lee faced a daunting, seemingly impossible challenge. McClellan had maneuvered nearly 100,000 troops to within seven miles of Richmond, three Union units were closing in on General Jackson's Confederates in Virginia's Shenandoah Valley, and a fourth Union army was camped on the Rappahannock River ostensibly ready to come to McClellan's aid. On June 12, as McClellan sat on Richmond's eastern outskirts waiting for reinforcements, Lee began to ring the city with troop entrenchments. Realizing that McClellan's flank appeared to be exposed, Lee tasked Stuart with assessing whether the Union army had any real protection north and west of the exposed flank. Stuart suggested that his men circumnavigate McClellan's army, to which Lee responded with deference that would become his trademark and a symbol of his trust in his subordinates. Lee gave Stuart vague orders:

"You will return as soon as the object of your expedition is accomplished, and you must bear constantly in mind, while endeavoring to execute the general purpose of your mission, not to hazard unnecessarily your command or to attempt what your judgment may not approve; but be content to accomplish all the good you can without feeling it necessary to obtain all that might be desired. I recommend that you take only such men as can stand the expedition, and that you take every means in your power to save and cherish those you take. You must leave sufficient cavalry here for the service of this army, and remember that one of the chief objects of your expedition is to gain intelligence for the guidance of future operations."

With that, Stuart embarked with 1200 troopers on a spectacular three-day, 150 mile ride in the rear of and around the entire Army of the Potomac, a mission that would require him to keep just ahead of pursuing horsemen led by Union Brig. General Philip St. George Cooke, Stuart's father-in-law. Though daunting and dangerous, Stuart and his men successfully completed the historic ride, with Stuart returning to Richmond to report to Lee on June 14 and most of his cavalry returning the following day. Stuart was able not only to report that McClellan's flank was indeed completely unguarded, he delivered 165 captured Union soldiers, 260 horses and mules, and a collection of quartermaster and ordinance supplies as well. The "ride around McClellan" proved to be a public relations sensation for Stuart, resulting in dramatic newspaper accounts, hordes of women cheering and strewing flower petals in his path when he rode through the streets of Richmond, and his face appearing on the front pages of most newspapers in both the North and South. The flamboyant officer relished every second of his ride, later writing, "There was something of the sublime in the implicit confidence and unquestioning trust of the rank and file in a leader guiding them straight, apparently, into the very jaws of the enemy, every step appearing to them to diminish the faintest hope of extrication."

Stuart also knew how to cultivate his newfound glory. When Stuart reported to General Lee, he also gave a verbal report to Virginia's governor, who rewarded him with a sword. During one visit to the governor, Stuart gave an impromptu address on the steps of the executive mansion to an assembling crowd, playfully telling them he "had been to the Chickahominy to visit some of his old friends of the United States Army, but they, very uncivilly, turned their backs upon him." The man who wrote the account of that speech also noted Stuart very conspicuously galloped off as the crowd cheered.

Although it was this kind of bombast that would come to color Stuart's legacy and in some ways eclipse his solid work, his men realized just how capable he was. In his 1887 memoirs, Colonel John Singleton Mosby (assigned as a first lieutenant to Stuart's cavalry scouts) wrote: "In his work on the outposts Stuart soon showed that he possessed the qualities of a great leader of cavalry. He never had an equal in such service. He discarded the old maxims and soon discovered that in the conditions of modern war the chief functions of cavalry are to learn the designs and to watch and report the movements of the enemy."[10] And for his own part, Stuart always reported which of his subordinates had distinguished themselves in post-battle reports.

Just a few weeks after Stuart's ride had put him on a pedestal with Jackson as the Confederacy's greatest heroes, Lee would join the pantheon. In a series of confrontations known as the Seven Days' Battle, Lee instructed Jackson to move as if to advance back through the Shenandoah Valley but then secretly bring his entire force by train back to the Richmond sector as reinforcements. Jackson had successfully tied up the Union armies in the Valley before returning to Richmond. Lee immediately took the offensive, attacking the Army of the Potomac repeatedly in a flurry of battles known as the Seven Days Battles. Fearing he was heavily outnumbered, McClellan began a strategic retreat, and despite badly defeating the Confederates at the Battle of Malvern Hill, the last battle of the Seven Days Battles and the Peninsula Campaign, it was clear that the Army of the Potomac was quitting the campaign. The failure of McClellan's campaign devastated the morale of the North, as McClellan had failed to advance despite originally having almost double the manpower.

In a characteristically audacious manner that came to define his generalship, Lee's bold offensive tactics had seen his army engage in bloody hand-to-hand combat that ranged from Mechanicsville to Fraser's Farm to Malvern Hill. By themselves, none of the battles could be called pivotal or even tactical victories for the Confederates, and Malvern Hill was a debacle, but from a strategic standpoint Lee succeeded in forcing McClellan and his back-up forces to retreat, while Jackson's tactics proved effective in the Shenandoah. Lee had prevented McClellan from capturing Richmond.

---

[10] Mosby, John Singleton. *The Memoirs of Colonel John S. Mosby.*

The Second Battle of Bull Run or Manassas

On July 25, 1862, after the conclusion of the Seven Days Battles had brought the Peninsula Campaign to an end, Stuart was promoted to Major General, his command upgraded to Cavalry Division. But Stuart and the Army of Northern Virginia were just getting started.

Even before McClellan had completely withdrawn his troops, Lee sent Jackson northward to intercept the new army Abraham Lincoln had placed under Maj. General John Pope, formed out of the scattered troops in the Virginia area. Pope had found success in the Western theater, and he was uncommonly brash, instructing the previously defeated men now under his command that his soldiers in the West were accustomed to seeing the backs of the enemy. Pope's arrogance turned off his own men, and it also caught the notice of the Confederates.

Once certain McClellan was in full retreat, Lee joined Jackson, planning to strike Pope before McClellan's troops could arrive as reinforcements. In late August 1862, in what is described in military annals as a "daring and unorthodox" move, Lee divided his forces and sent Jackson northward to flank them, ultimately bringing Jackson directly behind Pope's army and supply base. This forced Pope to fall back to Manassas to protect his flank and maintain his lines of communication. Recognizing Lee's genius for military strategy, General Jackson quickly became Lee's most trusted commander, and he would later say that he so trusted Lee's military instincts that he would even follow him into battle blindfolded.

In August 1862, Stuart completed yet another ride around the Union army, though this one was not as historic or memorable. On August 21, while conducting a series of highly-effective raids against Union forces, Stuart was nearly captured (and did lose his signature peacock plumed hat and cloak), but the following day managed to overrun Union commander Maj. General John Pope's headquarters during a raid on Catlett's Station, Virginia, not only capturing Pope's full uniform, but several staff officers and secret orders that provided Lee invaluable intelligence concerning troop reinforcements for Pope's army.

When Pope's army fell back to Manassas to confront Jackson, his wing of Lee's army dug in along a railroad trench and took a defensive stance. The Second Battle of Manassas or Bull Run was fought August 28-30, beginning with the Union army throwing itself at Jackson. While Jackson's men defended themselves, Lee used Longstreet's wing to deliver a devastating flank attack before reinforcements from the retreating Army of the Potomac could reach the field. The strategy, which came to be referred to as the "anvil and hammer", saw Longstreet's men sweep Pope's army off the field. Fought on the same ground as the First Battle of Manassas nearly a year earlier, the result was the same: a decisive Confederate victory that sent Union soldiers scrambling back to the safety of Washington.

General Longstreet, who Lee would later call his "Old Warhorse"

Jackson's cavalry followed the massive assault launched by Longstreet, while protecting its flank with artillery batteries. Stuart then ordered Brig. General Beverly Robertson to pursue Union General John Buford's cavalry brigade, many of whom were new to combat, as they retreated across Lewis's Ford, with Stuart's troops subsequently capturing over 300 of them. Stuart's men then harassed the retreating Union columns until the campaign ended at the Battle of Chantilly on September 1.

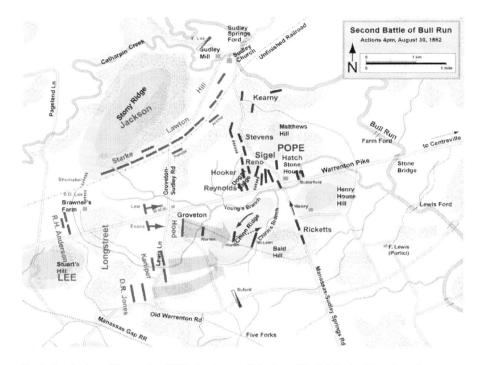

By the beginning of September 1862, the Army of Northern Virginia had achieved another major victory and now stood unopposed 12 miles away from Washington D.C. While Johnston and Beauregard had stayed in this position in the months after the first battle, Lee determined upon a more aggressive course: taking the fighting to the North.

The Maryland Campaign

In the summer of 1862, the Union suffered more than 20,000 casualties, and Northern Democrats, who had been split into pro-war and anti-war factions from the beginning, increasingly began to question the war. As of September 1862, no progress had been made on Richmond; in fact, a Confederate army was now in Maryland. And with the election of 1862 was approaching, Lincoln feared the Republicans might suffer losses in the congressional midterms that would harm the war effort. Thus, he restored General McClellan and removed General Pope after the second disaster at Bull Run. McClellan was still immensely popular among the Army of the Potomac, and with a mixture of men from his Army of the Potomac and Pope's Army of Virginia, he began a cautious pursuit of Lee into Maryland.

In early September, convinced that the best way to defend Richmond was to divert attention to Washington, Lee had decided to invade Maryland after obtaining Jefferson Davis's permission. Today the decision is remembered through the prism of Lee hoping to win a major battle in the North that would bring about European recognition of the Confederacy, potential intervention, and possible capitulation by the North, whose anti-war Democrats were picking up political momentum. However, Lee also hoped that the fighting in Maryland would relieve Virginia's resources, especially the Shenandoah Valley, which served as the state's "breadbasket". And though largely forgotten today, Lee's move was controversial among his own men. Confederate soldiers, including Lee, took up arms to defend their homes, but now they were being asked to invade a Northern state. An untold number of Confederate soldiers refused to cross the Potomac River into Maryland.

Historians believe that Lee's entire Army of Northern Virginia had perhaps 50,000 men at most and possibly closer to 30,000 during the Maryland campaign. However, Lee sized up George McClellan, figured he was a cautious general, and decided once again to divide his forces throughout Maryland. In early September, he ordered Jackson to capture Harpers Ferry while he and Longstreet maneuvered his troops toward Frederick. With McClellan now assuming command of the Northern forces, Lee expected to have plenty of time to assemble his troops and bring his battle plan to fruition.

Now officially designated the "Eyes of the Army," in September of 1862, Stuart committed what many military historians deem his first tactical error when, for a five-day period at the beginning of the Maryland Campaign, he rested his men and entertained local civilians at a gala ball at Urbana, Maryland rather than keep the Union enemy under surveillance. With no incoming intelligence, Lee was unaware of Union General McClellan's location and the speed at which his forces approached.

This error was magnified by the fact that the North had just had one of the greatest strokes of luck during the Civil War. For reasons that are still unclear, Union troops in camp at Frederick came across a copy of Special Order 191, wrapped up among three cigars. The order contained Lee's entire marching plans for Maryland, making it clear that the Army of Northern Virginia had been divided into multiple parts, which, if faced by overpowering strength, could be entirely defeated and bagged. The "Lost Order" quickly made its way to General McClellan, who took several hours to debate whether or not it was intentional misinformation or actually real. Once he decided it was accurate, McClellan is said to have famously boasted, "Here is a paper with which if I cannot whip Bobby Lee, I will be willing to go home."

To Lee's and Stuart's great surprise, McClellan's army began moving at an uncharacteristically quick pace, pushing in on Confederate forces at several mountain passes at South Mountain, including at Turner's Gap and Crampton's Gap. Stuart's men arrived in time to skirmish at various points but were unable to resist the Union's well-organized offensive. Moreover, Stuart had misjudged the Union Army's approach routes, and was unaware of its advance against Turner's Gap at South Mountain near Middletown. While Jackson's wing was forcing the Harpers Ferry garrison to surrender, Lee was forced to regather his other scattered units around Sharpsburg near Antietam Creek. McClellan's army, which may have outnumbered Lee's forces by about 50,000 men, confronted the Confederates around the night of September 16. Although an immediate Union attack on the morning of September 16 would have nearly guaranteed a McClellan victory due to his overwhelming numbers, his belief that Lee had as many as 100,000 camped at Sharpsburg (though his numbers were closer to 38,000) prompted him to hesitate.

As fate would have it, the bloodiest day in the history of the United States took place on the 75th anniversary of the signing of the Constitution. On September 17, 1862, Lee's Army of Northern Virginia fought McClellan's Army of the Potomac outside Sharpsburg along Antietam Creek. That day, nearly 25,000 would become casualties, and Lee's army barely survived fighting the much bigger Northern army. The fighting that morning started with savage fighting on the Confederate left flank near Dunker church, in a corn field and forests, with the Confederates barely held the field in the north sector. McClellan ordered General Joseph Hooker's I Corps to cross Antietam Creek and lead the attacks against the enemy positions, while General Meade's division attacked the Confederates near the East Woods and McClellan continued to bring his troops into position. McClellan planned to overwhelm the Confederate's left flank by utilizing the physical configuration of the bridges over the Antietam. Stuart was ordered to bombard the Union flank as it opened its attack, but by mid-afternoon, was redirected by "Stonewall" Jackson to command a turning movement against the Union right flank and rear.

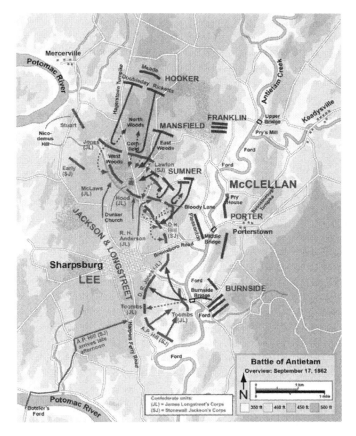

Lee's army may have been saved by the Northern army's inability to cross the creek near "Burnside's Bridge". Ambrose Burnside had been given command of the "Right Wing" of the Army of the Potomac (the I Corps and IX Corps) at the start of the Maryland Campaign for the Battle of South Mountain, but McClellan separated the two corps at the Battle of Antietam, placing them on opposite ends of the Union battle line. However, Burnside continued to act as though he was a wing commander instead of a corps commander, so instead of ordering the IX corps, he funneled orders through General Jacob D. Cox. This poor organization contributed to the corps's hours-long delay in attacking and crossing what is now called "Burnside's Bridge" on the right flank of the Confederate line.

General Burnside

Making matters worse, Burnside did not perform adequate reconnaissance of the area, which had several easy fording sites of the creek out of range of the Army of Northern Virginia. Instead of unopposed crossings, his troops were forced into repeated assaults across the narrow bridge which was dominated by Confederate sharpshooters on high ground across the bridge. The delay allowed General A.P. Hill's Confederate division to reach the battlefield from Harpers Ferry in time to save Lee's right flank that afternoon. Fearing that his army was badly bloodied and figuring Lee had many more men than he did, McClellan refused to commit his reserves to continue the attacks. The day ended in a tactical stalemate.

On the morning of September 18, Lee's army prepared to defend against a Union assault that ultimately never came. Finally, an improvised truce was declared to allow both sides to exchange their wounded. That evening, Lee's forces began withdrawing across the Potomac to return to Virginia, with McClellan, surprisingly, opting not to pursue, citing shortages of equipment and the fear of overextending his forces. Nevertheless, Antietam is now widely considered a turning point in the war. Although the battle was tactically a draw, it resulted in forcing Lee's army out of Maryland and back into Virginia, making it a strategic victory for the North and an opportune time for President Abraham Lincoln to issue the Emancipation Proclamation.

Once the Army of Northern Virginia was safely back in Virginia, Stuart executed another of his daring circumnavigations of the Army of the Potomac, this time traveling 120 miles in under 60 hours. Once again he had embarrassed his Union opponents while seizing horses and supplies. Afterwards, Stuart gifted "Stonewall" Jackson a fine, new officer's tunic, trimmed with gold lace, commissioned from a Richmond tailor, which he thought would give Jackson more of a "proper" general appearance--a gift to which Jackson was famously indifferent and almost always refuse to wore (with the exception of his last official portrait, which was taken less than two weeks before Chancellorsville). And while these exploits proved only marginally significant (resulting in little military advantage), when word reached the newspapers, they did much to boost Southern morale.

Even then, it did not escape the notice of observers that Stuart and Jackson were an odd couple, and Jackson biographer James Robertson Jr. later wrote, "Stuart and Jackson were an unlikely pair: one outgoing, the other introverted; one flashily uniformed, the other plainly dressed; one Prince Rupert and the other Cromwell. Yet Stuart's self-confidence, penchant for action, deep love of Virginia, and total abstinence from such vices as alcohol, tobacco, and pessimism endeared him to Jackson... Stuart was the only man in the Confederacy who could make Jackson laugh—and who dared to do so."

Despite heavily outnumbering the Southern army and badly damaging it during the battle of Antietam, McClellan never did pursue Lee across the Potomac, citing shortages of equipment and the fear of overextending his forces. General-in-Chief Henry W. Halleck wrote in his official report, "The long inactivity of so large an army in the face of a defeated foe, and during the most favorable season for rapid movements and a vigorous campaign, was a matter of great disappointment and regret." Lincoln had also had enough of McClellan's "slows", and his constant excuses for not taking forward action. Lincoln relieved McClellan of his command of the Army of the Potomac on November 7, 1862, effectively ending the general's military career.

The Fredericksburg Campaign

In place of McClellan, Lincoln appointed Burnside, who had just failed at Antietam. Burnside didn't believe he was competent to command the entire army, a very honest (and accurate) judgment. However, Burnside also didn't want the command to fall upon Joe Hooker, who had been injured while aggressively fighting with his I Corps at Antietam in the morning. Thus, he accepted.

Under pressure from Lincoln to be aggressive, Burnside laid out a difficult plan to cross the Rappahannock and attack the Confederates near Fredericksburg. The plan was doomed from the very beginning. On December 12, Burnside's army struggled to cross the river under fire from Confederate sharpshooters in the town.

The majority of the fighting took place the next day, and the most contested fighting found Stuart and his men in the thick of it on the Confederates' right flank. Maj General Stuart and his cavalry—more specifically, his horse artillery under Major John Pelham—protected "Stonewall" Jackson's flank when it came under attack from General William B. Franklin. Franklin's "grand division" was able to penetrate General Jackson's defensive line to the south, but it was ultimately driven back. After the battle, General Lee commended Stuart's cavalry which, in his words, "effectually guarded our right, annoying the enemy and embarrassing his movements by hanging on his flank and attacking when the opportunity occurred."[11] Stuart informed his wife

Flora that he had been shot through his fur collar during the encounter, but was otherwise unhurt.

Although the fighting was fierce there, the battle is mostly remembered for the piecemeal attacks the Union army made on heavily fortified positions Longstreet's men took up on Marye's Heights. The Northern soldiers were mowed down again and again, and the Union would suffer twice as many casualties as the Confederates during the battle, making it one of the most lopsided major battles of the Civil War.

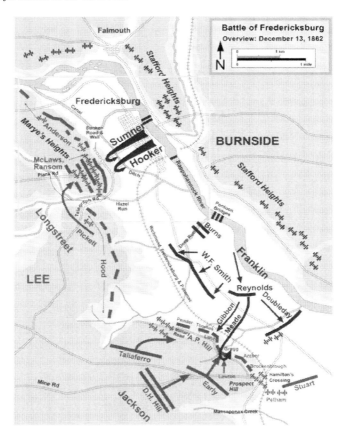

As men lay dying on the field that night, the Northern Lights made a rare appearance. Southern

11   Wert, Jeffry D. *Cavalryman of the Lost Cause: A Biography of J.E.B. Stuart.* Page 193.

soldiers took it as a divine omen and wrote about it frequently in their diaries. The Union soldiers saw less divine inspiration in the Northern Lights and mentioned it less in their own. The Battle of Fredericksburg also spawned one of Lee's most memorable quotes. During the battle, Lee turned to Longstreet and commented, "It is well that war is so terrible, otherwise we would grow too fond of it."[12]

In the final weeks of 1862, Stuart led a raid north of the Rappahannock River, inflicting some 230 casualties while losing only 27 of his own men.

Chapter 6: 1863

The Chancellorsville Campaign

Fredericksburg had concluded an incredibly successful year for the Confederates in the East, but the South was still struggling. The Confederate forces in the West had failed to win a major battle, suffering defeat at places like Shiloh in Tennessee and across the Mississippi River. As the war continued into 1863, the southern economy continued to deteriorate. Southern armies were suffering serious deficiencies of nearly all supplies as the Union blockade continued to be effective as stopping most international commerce with the Confederacy. Moreover, the prospect of Great Britain or France recognizing the Confederacy had been all but eliminated by the Emancipation Proclamation.

Given the unlikelihood of forcing the North's capitulation, the Confederacy's main hope for victory was to win some decisive victory or hope that Abraham Lincoln would lose his reelection bid in 1864, and that the new president would want to negotiate peace with the Confederacy. Understandably, this colored Confederate war strategy, and unquestionably Lee's.

After the Fredericksburg debacle and the "Mud March" fiasco that left a Union advance literally dead in its tracks, Lincoln fired Burnside and replaced him with "Fighting Joe" Hooker. Hooker had gotten his nickname from a clerical error in a newspaper's description of fighting, but the nickname stuck, and Lee would later playfully refer to him as F.J. Hooker. Hooker had stood out for his zealous fighting at Antietam, and the battle may very well have turned out differently if he hadn't been injured at the head of the I Corps early that morning. Now he was in command of a 100,000 man Army of the Potomac, and he devised a complex plan to cross the Rappahannock River with part of his force near Fredericksburg to pin down Lee while using the other bulk to turn Lee's left, which would allow his forces to reach the Confederate rear.

Hooker's plan initially worked perfectly, with the division of his army surprising Lee. Lee was

---

12   Nagel, Paul C. *The Lee's of Virginia.* Page 179.

outnumbered two to one and now had to worry about threats on two fronts. Incredibly, Lee once again decided to divide his forces in the face of the enemy, sending Stonewall Jackson's corps to turn the Union army's right flank while the rest of the army maintained positions near Fredericksburg. It would fall upon Stuart and his cavalry to screen Jackson's movement, which if fully discovered could have been fatal for the Confederates.

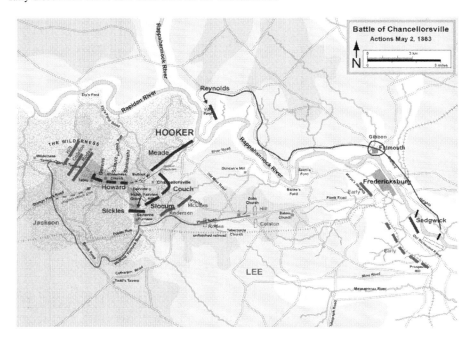

The Battle of Chancellorsville is one of the most famous of the Civil War, and the most famous part of the battle was Stonewall Jackson's daring march across the Army of the Potomac's flank, surprising the XI Corps with an attack on May 2, 1863. Having ignored warnings of Jackson's march, the XI Corps was quickly routed. The surprise was a costly success however. Jackson scouted out ahead of his lines later that night and was mistakenly fired upon by his own men, badly wounding him. Jackson's natural replacement, A.P. Hill, was also injured

Bypassing the next most-senior infantry general in the corps, Brig. General Robert E. Rodes directed Stuart himself to take temporary command of the Second Infantry Corps, a decision Lee seconded when news reached him. Although this change in command effectively ended the flanking attack underway, Stuart proved to be a remarkably adaptive leader and very effective infantry commander, launching a successful, well-coordinated assault against the Union right flank at Chancellorsville the following day. Meanwhile on the other flank, the Confederates evacuated from Fredericksburg but ultimately held the line. Hooker began to lose his nerve, and he was injured during the battle when a cannonball nearly killed him. Historians now believe that Hooker may have commanded part of the battle while suffering from a concussion.

   On May 4, as Hooker abandoned the high ground at Hazel Grove in favor of Fairview, Stuart showed particular acumen by immediately taking control of the position and ordering thirty pieces of artillery to bombard the Union positions, not only forcing General Hooker's troops from Fairview (which Stuart then captured for the Confederacy), but essentially decimating the Union lines while destroying Hooker's headquarters at Chancellor House. Of this well-played turn of events, Stuart wrote: "As the sun lifted the mist that shrouded the field, it was discovered that the ridge on the extreme right was a fine position for concentrating artillery. I immediately ordered thirty pieces to that point, and, under the happy effects of the battalion system, it was done quickly. The effect of this fire upon the enemy's batteries was superb."[13]

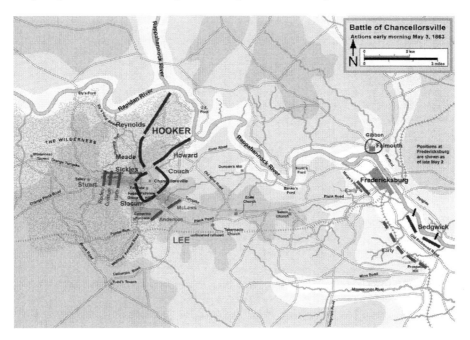

Stuart's effective utilization of a mere 20,000 men to snatch victory from a Union force

---

[13]   See: Stuart Family Archives.

numbering over 80,000 prompted Confederate General Porter Alexander to comment, "Altogether, I do not think there was a more brilliant thing done in the war than Stuart's extricating that command from the extremely critical position in which he found it."[14] Some historians have speculated that Stuart's success at Hazel Grove was what induced Dan Sickles to disobey George Meade's orders on Day 2 at Gettysburg and advance his III Corps a mile out in front of the rest of the Union line to occupy high ground. Perhaps fearful of a replay like Chancellorsville, that fateful decision would dominate the fighting on the second day of the war's greatest battle.

Brandy Station: The Biggest Cavalry Battle of the War

By the end of the Battle of Chancellorsville, the Army of the Potomac had once again been defeated, retreating across the river. But Lee would also lose his "right hand". After Jackson's left arm was amputated, he seemed to be recovering, but his doctors were unaware of his symptoms that indicated oncoming pneumonia. Jackson would die on May 10, eight days after his brilliant attack.

In the spring of 1863, General Lee discovered that McClellan had known of his plans and was able to force a battle at Antietam before all of General Lee's forces had arrived. General Lee now believed that he could successfully invade the North again, and that his defeat before was due in great measure to a stroke of bad luck. In addition, General Lee hoped to supply his army on the unscathed fields and towns of the North, while giving war ravaged northern Virginia a rest.

Knowing that victories on Virginia soil meant little to an enemy that could simply retreat, regroup, and then return with more men and more advanced equipment, Lee set his sights on a Northern invasion, aiming to turn Northern opinion against the war and against President Lincoln. With his men already half-starved from dwindling provisions, Lee intended to confiscate food, horses, and equipment as they pushed north--and hopefully influence Northern politicians into giving up their support of the war by penetrating into Harrisburg or even Philadelphia. Given the right circumstances, Lee's army might even be able to capture either Baltimore or Philadelphia and use the city as leverage in peace negotiations.

In early June, the Army of Northern Virginia occupied Culpeper, Virginia. After their victories at Fredericksburg and Chancellorsville against armies twice their size, Confederate troops felt invincible and anxious to carry the war north into Pennsylvania. Assuming his role as Lee's "Eyes of the Army" for the Pennsylvania Campaign, Stuart bivouacked his men near the Rappahannock River, screening the Confederate Army against surprise Union attacks. Taken with his recent successes, Stuart requested a full field review of his units by General Lee, and on June 8, paraded his nearly 9,000 mounted troops and four batteries of horse artillery for review,

---

[14]   Wert, Jeffry D. *Cavalryman of the Lost Cause: A Biography of J.E.B. Stuart*. Page 223.

also charging in simulated battle at Inlet Station about two miles southwest of Brandy Station. While Lee himself was unavailable to attend the review, some of the cavalrymen and newspaper reporters at the scene complained that all Stuart was doing was "feeding his ego and exhausting the horses." He began to be referred to as a "headline-hunting show-off."

Despite the critics, Stuart basked in the glory. Renowned Civil War historian Stephen Sears described the scene, "The grand review of June 5 was surely the proudest day of Jeb Stuart's thirty years. As he led a cavalcade of resplendent staff officers to the reviewing stand, trumpeters heralded his coming and women and girls strewed his path with flowers. Before all of the spectators the assembled cavalry brigade stretched a mile and a half. After Stuart and his entourage galloped past the line in review, the troopers in their turn saluted the reviewing stand in columns of squadrons. In performing a second "march past," the squadrons started off at a trot, then spurred to a gallop. Drawing sabers and breaking into the Rebel yell, the troopers rush toward the horse artillery drawn up in battery. The gunners responded defiantly, firing blank charges. Amidst this tumult of cannon fire and thundering hooves, a number of ladies swooned in their escorts' arms."[15]

However much Stuart enjoyed "horsing around", there was serious work to be done. The following day, Lee ordered Stuart to cross the Rappahannock and raid Union forward positions, shielding the Confederate Army from observation or interference as it moved north. Already anticipating this imminent offensive move, Stuart had ordered his troops back into formation around Brandy Station. Here, Stuart would endure the first of two low points in his military career: the Battle of Brandy Station, the largest predominantly cavalry engagement of the Civil War.

Union Maj. General Joseph Hooker interpreted Stuart's presence around Culpeper as a precursor to a raid on his army's supply lines. In response, he ordered his cavalry commander, Maj. General Alfred Pleasonton, to take a combined force of 8,000 cavalry and 3,000 infantry on a raid to "disperse and destroy" the 9,500 Confederates. Crossing the Rappahannock River in two columns on June 9, 1863 at Beverly's Ford and Kelly's Ford, the first infantry unit caught Stuart completely off-guard, and the second surprised him yet again. Suddenly the Confederates were being battered both front and rear by mounted Union troops.

---

[15]   Sears, Stephen W. *Gettysburg*. Page 64.

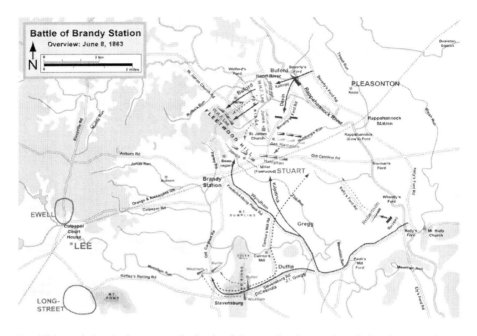

In addition to being the largest cavalry battle of the war, the chaos and confusion that ensued across the battlefield also made Brandy Station unique in that most of the fighting was done while mounted and using sabers. One account of the battle noted, "Of the bodies that littered the field that day, the vast majority were found to have perished by the sword."

After ten hours of charges and countercharges that swept back and forth across Fleetwood Hill (where Stuart had headquartered the night before) involving drawn sabers and revolvers, Pleasonton decided to withdraw his exhausted men across the Rappahannock River. Stuart immediately claimed a Confederate victory because his men had managed to hold the field and inflicted more casualties on the enemy while forcing Pleasonton to withdraw before locating Lee's infantry. But Stuart was trying to save face, and nobody else, including Lee, took his view of the battle. The fact was, the Southern cavalry under Stuart had not detected the movement of two large columns of Union cavalry and had fallen prey to not one but *two* surprise attacks. Two days later the Richmond *Enquirer* reported: "If Gen. Stuart is to be the eyes and ears of the army we advise him to see more, and be seen less. Gen. Stuart has suffered no little in public estimation by the late enterprises of the enemy."[16]

---

[16]   Wert, Jeffry D. *Cavalryman of the Lost Cause: A Biography of J.E.B. Stuart.* Page 251.

Lee was now painfully aware of the increased competency of the Union cavalry, as well as the decline of the seemingly once-invincible Southern mounted armed forces under Stuart.

The Gettysburg Campaign

As a result of recent battles, several Confederate generals had important objectives entering the Gettysburg campaign. In the wake of Jackson's death, Lee reorganized his army, creating three Corps out of the previous two, with A.P. Hill and Richard S. Ewell "replacing" Stonewall. Hill had been a successful division commander, but he was constantly battling bouts of sickness that left him disabled, which would occur at Gettysburg. Ewell had distinguished himself during the Peninsula Campaign, suffering a serious injury that historians often credit as making him more cautious in command upon his return.

With Stuart's cavalry screening his movements, Lee marched his army into Pennsylvania looking for some sort of coup de grace that could strike a mortal blow to the North. Once again, Lee divided his forces to take different objectives, but this time they stayed within a day's marching distance of each other to avoid a repeat of the near disaster at Antietam. Meanwhile, the loss at Chancellorsville led to Lincoln relieving Hooker as he was leading the Army of the Potomac in pursuit of Lee. George Meade assumed command of the Army of the Potomac just a few days before the Battle of Gettysburg.

During the first weeks of summer of 1863, as Stuart screened the army and completed several well-executed offenses against Union cavalry, many historians think it likely that he had already planned to remove the negative effect of Brandy Station by duplicating one of his now famous circumnavigating rides around the enemy army. But as Lee began his march north through the Shenandoah Valley in western Virginia, it is highly unlikely that is what he wanted or expected.

Before setting out on June 22, the methodical Lee gave Stuart specific instructions as to the role he was to play in the Pennsylvania offensive: as the "Eyes of the Army" he was to guard the mountain passes with part of his force while the Army of Northern Virginia was still south of the Potomac River, and then cross the river with the remainder of his army and screen the right flank of Confederate general Richard Stoddert Ewell's Second Corps as it moved down the Shenandoah Valley, maintaining contact with Ewell's army as it advanced towards Harrisburg.

But instead of taking the most direct route north near the Blue Ridge Mountains, Stuart chose a much more ambitious course of action.

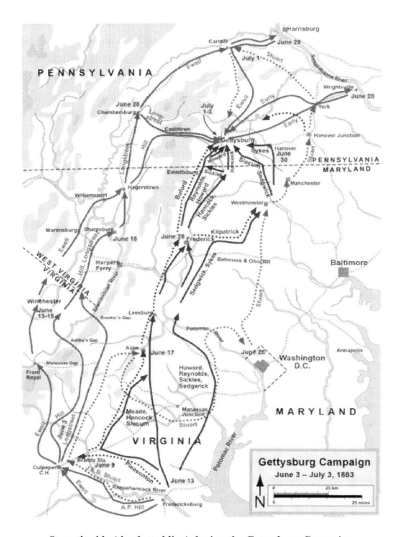

Stuart's ride (the dotted line) during the Gettysburg Campaign

Stuart decided to march his three best brigades (under Generals Hampton and Fitzhugh Lee, and Col. John R. Chambliss) between the Union army and Washington, north through Rockville to Westminster, and then into Pennsylvania--a route that would allow them to capture supplies along the way and wreak havoc as they skirted Washington. In the aftermath, the *Washington Star* would write: "The cavalry chief [Stuart] interpreted his marching orders in a way that best suited his nature, and detached his 9000 troopers from their task of screening the main army and keeping tabs on the Federals. When Lee was in Pennsylvania anxiously looking for him, Stuart crossed the Potomac above Washington and captured a fine prize of Federal supply wagons . . . ."[17]

But to complicate matters even more, as Stuart set out on June 25 on what was probably a glory-seeking mission, he was unaware that his intended path was blocked by columns of Union infantry that would invariably force him to veer farther east than he or Lee had anticipated. Ultimately, his decision would prevent him from linking up with Ewell as ordered and deprive Lee of his primary cavalry force as he advanced deeper and deeper into unfamiliar enemy territory. According to Halsey Wigfall (son of Confederate States Senator Louis Wigfall) who was in Stuart's infantry, "Stuart and his cavalry left [Lee's] army on June 24 and did not contact [his] army again until the afternoon of July 2, the second day of the [Gettysburg] battle."[18]

According to Stuart's own account, on June 29 his men clashed briefly with two companies of Union cavalry in Westminster, Maryland, overwhelming and chasing them "a long distance on the Baltimore road," causing a "great panic" in the city of Baltimore. On June 30, the head of Stuart's column then encountered Union Brig. General Judson Kilpatrick's cavalry as it passed through Hanover--reportedly capturing a wagon train and scattering the Union army--after which Kilpatrick's men were able to regroup and drive Stuart and his men out of town. Then after a twenty-mile trek in the dark, Stuart's exhausted men reached Dover, Pennsylvania, on the morning of July 1 (which they briefly occupied).

Given great discretion in his cavalry operations before the battle, Stuart's cavalry was too far removed from the Army of Northern Virginia to warn Lee of the Army of the Potomac's movements. As it would turn out, Lee's army inadvertently stumbled into Union cavalry and then the Union army at Gettysburg on the morning of July 1, 1863, walking blindly into what became the largest battle of the war. One of Longstreet's spies had warned the Confederates that the Union army was in Pennsylvania, but Lee was unaware of their placement when an advanced division of A.P. Hill's Corps marched toward Gettysburg on the morning of July 1. The battle began with John Buford's cavalry forces skirmishing against the advancing division of Heth's just outside of town. Buford's actions allowed the I Corps of the Army of the Potomac to reach Gettysburg and engage the Confederates, eventually setting the stage for the biggest and most well known battle of the war.

---

[17]   Stepp, John W. & Hill, William I. (editors), *Mirror of War, the Washington Star reports the Civil War*. Page 199.
[18]   Eaton, Clement. *Jefferson Davis*. Page 178.

Day 1 by itself would have been one of the 20 biggest battles of the Civil War, and it was a tactical Confederate victory. While the Army of the Potomac's I and XI Corps engaged in heavy fighting, they were eventually flanked from the north by Ewell's Corps, which was returning toward Gettysburg from its previous objective. After a disorderly retreat through the town itself, the Union men began to dig in on high ground to the southeast of the town.

It was at this point that Lee arrived on the field and saw the importance of this position. He sent discretionary orders to Ewell that Cemetery Hill be taken "if practicable." Ewell chose not to attempt the assault. Lee's order has been criticized because it left too much discretion to Ewell, leaving historians to speculate on how the more aggressive Stonewall Jackson would have acted on this order if he had lived to command this wing of Lee's army, and how differently the second day of battle would have proceeded with Confederate possession of Culp's Hill or Cemetery Hill. Discretionary orders were customary for General Lee because Jackson and Longstreet, his other principal subordinate, usually reacted to them aggressively and used their initiative to act quickly and forcefully. Ewell's decision not to attack, whether justified or not, may have ultimately cost the Confederates the battle.

General Ewell

With so many men engaged and now taking refuge on the high ground, Meade, who was an engineer like Lee, abandoned his previous plan to draw up a defensive line around Emmittsburg a few miles to the South. After a council of war, the Army of the Potomac determined to defend at Gettysburg.

On the morning of Day 2, Lee decided to attempt attacks on both Union flanks, ordering

Ewell's corps to attack Culp's Hill on the Union right while Longstreet's corps would attack on the Union left.

As it turned out, both attacks would come too late. Though there was a controversy over when Lee ordered Longstreet's attack, Longstreet's march got tangled up and caused several hours of delay. The delay would ultimately allow the Army of the Potomac to move men onto Little Round Top, high ground that commanded much of the field. Longstreet's and Hill's men smashed the Union soldiers, particularly the III Corps, which commander Dan Sickles had moved forward nearly a mile against Meade's orders. The salient in the Union army's line led to much of the effort of the attack taking place there, and the North was able to hold off the attacks against Little Round Top.

Meanwhile, Ewell's attack against Culp's Hill on the other end of the field met with some success in pushing the Army of the Potomac back. However, the attack started so late in the day that nightfall made it impossible for the Confederates to capitalize on their success. Ewell's men would spend the night at the base of Culp's Hill and partially up the hill, but it would fall upon them to pick up the attack the next morning.

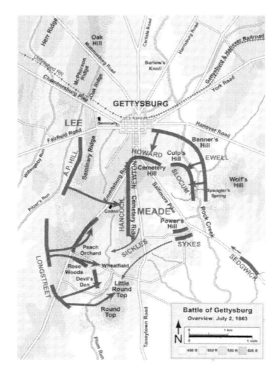

Battle of Gettysburg
Overview: July 2, 1863

That night, Meade held another council of war. Having been attacked on both flanks, Meade and his top officers correctly surmised that Lee would attempt an attack on the center of the line the next day. Moreover, captured Confederates and the fighting and intelligence of Day 2 let it be known that the only Confederate unit that had not yet seen action during the fighting was George Pickett's division of Longstreet's corps.

General Meade

Late on the second day of the battle, Stuart finally arrived, bringing with him the caravan of captured Union supply wagons, and he was immediately reprimanded by Lee. One account describes Lee as "visibly angry" raising his hand "as if to strike the tardy cavalry commander."[19] While that does not sound like Lee's style, Stuart has been heavily criticized ever since, and it has been speculated Lee took him to task harshly enough that Stuart offered his resignation. Lee didn't accept it, but he would later note in his after battle report that the cavalry had not updated him as to the Army of the Potomac's movements.

On the morning of July 3, the Confederate attack against Culp's Hill fizzled out, but by then Lee had already planned a massive attack on the Union center, combined with having Stuart's cavalry attack the Union army's lines in the rear. A successful attack would split the Army of the Potomac at the same time its communication and supply lines were severed by Stuart, which would make it possible to capture the entire army in detail.

There was just one problem with the plan, as Longstreet told Lee that morning: no 15,000 men who ever existed could successfully execute the attack. The charge required marching across an open field for about a mile, with the Union artillery holding high ground on all sides of the incoming Confederates. Longstreet ardently opposed the attack, but, already two days into the battle, Lee explained that because the Army of the Potomac was here on the field, he must strike at it.

---

[19]   Philips, David. *Crucial Land Battles*. Page 75.

Realizing the insanity of sending 15,000 men hurtling into all the Union artillery, Lee planned to use the Confederate artillery to try to knock out the Union artillery ahead of time. Although old friend William Pendleton was the artillery chief, the artillery cannonade would be supervised by Edward Porter Alexander, Longstreet's chief artillerist, who would have to give the go-ahead to the charging infantry because they were falling under Longstreet's command.

From the beginning, the plan was an abject failure. Stuart's men did not defeat the Union cavalry and thus had no success. At East Cavalry Field, the Union cavalry fought the Confederate cavalry to a standstill, with George Custer's brigade of Michigan "Wolverines" bearing the brunt of the casualties.

Meanwhile, the Confederate artillery missed their mark. The artillery duel could be heard from dozens of miles away, and all the smoke led to Confederate artillery constantly overshooting their targets. Eventually, Union artillery chief Henry Hunt cleverly figured that if the Union cannons stopped firing back, the Confederates might think they successfully knocked out the Union batteries. On top of that, the Union would be preserving its ammunition for the impending charge that everyone now knew was coming.

Today Pickett's Charge is remembered as the American version of the Charge of the Light Brigade, a heroic but completely futile march that had no chance of success. In fact, it's remembered as Pickett's Charge because Pickett's Virginians wanted to claim the glory of getting the furthest during the attack in the years after the war. The charge consisted of about 15,000 men under the command of James Longstreet, with three divisions spearheaded by Pickett, Trimble, and Pettigrew. Trimble and Pettigrew were leading men from A.P. Hill's corps, and Hill was too disabled by illness that day to choose the men from his corps to make the charge. As a result, some of the men who charged that day had already engaged in heavy fighting.

Longstreet was so sure of disaster that he could barely take it upon himself to order the men ahead. He was right. The charge suffered about a 50% casualty rate, as the Confederates marched into hell. The men barely made a dent in the Union line before retreating in disorder back across the field, where Lee met them in an effort to regroup them in case the Union counterattacked. At one point, Lee ordered Pickett to reform his division, to which Pickett reportedly cried, "I have no division!"

General Pickett

After the South had lost the war, the importance of Gettysburg as one of the "high tide" marks of the Confederacy became apparent to everyone, making the battle all the more important in the years after it had been fought. Former Confederate comrades like Longstreet and Jubal Early would go on to argue who was responsible for the loss at Gettysburg (and thus the war) in the following decades. Much of the debate was fueled by those who wanted to protect Lee's legacy, especially because Lee was dead and could not defend himself in writing anymore. However, on July 3, Lee insisted on taking full blame for what occurred at Gettysburg, telling his retreating men, "It's all my fault." Historians have mostly agreed, placing the blame for the disastrous Day 3 on Lee's shoulders. Porter Alexander would later call it Lee's "worst day" of the war.

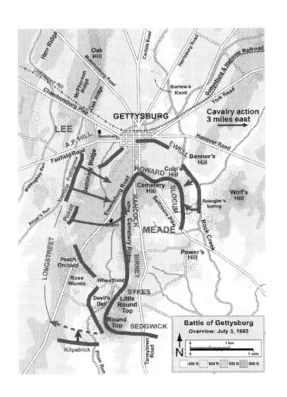

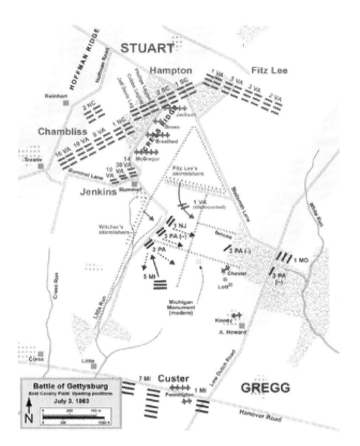

Though credited with devoting his full attention to the Confederate cause upon his arrival, many historians attribute the catastrophic loss to the absence of Stuart and his cavalry. Immediately becoming the most devastating event of Stuart's military career, in his official report General Lee's wrote, " . . . the absence of the cavalry rendered it impossible to obtain accurate information. By the route [we] pursued, the Federal Army was interposed between [my] command and our main body, preventing any communication with [Stuart] until his arrival at Carlisle. The march toward Gettysburg was conducted more slowly than it would have been had the movements of the Federal Army been known." Some of Stuart's subordinates would come to his defense after the war, and Lee deserves some blame for allowing his subordinates so much discretion, which may have worked with Stonewall Jackson but backfired spectacularly with Ewell and Stuart. After the war, Stuart's subordinate, General Thomas L. Rosser stated what many were already convinced of, "On this campaign, [Stuart] undoubtedly, make the fatal blunder which lost us the battle of Gettysburg."[20]

The End of 1863

By September 9, 1863, General Lee had reorganized his cavalry, creating a cavalry corps for Stuart with two divisions of three brigades each. In the Bristoe Campaign (in Virginia), Stuart was assigned to lead a broad turning movement in an attempt to access General Meade's rear, but Meade skillfully withdrew his army without providing the opportunity. On October 13, Stuart stumbled into the rear guard of the Union III Corps near Warrenton, resulting in Lee having to send General Ewell's corps to rescue him; Stuart managed to hide his troopers in a wooded ravine until the unsuspecting III Corps moved on. And then on October 14, as Meade withdrew towards Manassas Junction, brigades from the Union II Corps fought a rearguard action against Stuart's cavalry and a division of Brig. General Harry Hays near Auburn, with Stuart's cavalry effectively bluffing Union General Gouverneur K. Warren's infantry and narrowly evading disaster.

After the Confederate debacle at Bristoe Station and an aborted advance on Centreville, Virginia, Stuart's cavalry shielded the withdrawal of Lee's army from Manassas Junction, after which Union General Judson Kilpatrick's cavalry pursued Stuart's cavalry along the Warrenton Turnpike--but were lured into an ambush near Chestnut Hill and routed. Kilpatrick was the one Civil War officer who may have been even more flamboyant than Stuart.

And in a confrontation fought on October 19, 1863 that became known as the "Buckland Races" (and likened to a fox hunt), Stuart and Maj. General Wade Hampton's cavalry succeeded in not only routing Kilpatrick's cavalry, they pursued it at full-gallop for five miles to Haymarket and Gainesville, eventually forcing it to scatter. At this point, the Southern press began to reconsider its harsh criticism of Stuart.

When Lee had retreated from Pennsylvania without much fight from the Army of the Potomac, Lincoln was again discouraged, believing Meade had a chance to end the war if he had been bolder. Though historians dispute that, and the Confederates actually invited attack during their retreat, Lincoln was constantly looking for more aggressive fighters to lead his men. Lincoln had found one in Ulysses S. Grant, once famously explaining, "I cannot spare this man. He fights." Grant had led Union forces to several victories out west, including the siege of Vicksburg that split the Confederacy in two and gave the North complete control of the Mississippi. Now, Lincoln called Grant east to be commander in chief of all armies, while William Tecumseh Sherman became the principal commander in the West.

---

20   Wert, Jeffry D. *Cavalryman of the Lost Cause: A Biography of J.E.B. Stuart*. Page 300.

Chapter 7: 1864

The Battle of the Wilderness

By 1864, the South's war strategy was simply to ensure Lincoln lost reelection that November. With Grant's appointment, Lee now intended only to stand between Grant's army and Richmond, the heart of the Confederacy. And with virtually unlimited manpower and resources at his dispose, Grant need not be concerned with the cost of an all-out advance.

In April, Grant attached himself to Meade's Army of the Potomac and began marching it to meet Lee's army. On May 4, 1864, Grant launched what has come to be known as the Overland Campaign, during which he crossed the Rapidan River with 100,000 men near Fredericksburg. Grant's aims were simple: advance toward Richmond while fighting the enemy wherever he was. Lee could only assemble 60,000 men to meet the oncoming Army of the Potomac, and Grant's aggressive nature and advantage in manpower deprived Lee of any real ability to take a strategic initiative.

Nevertheless, Lee proved more than capable on the defensive. From May 5-6, Lee's men won a tactical victory at the Battle of the Wilderness, which was fought so close to where the Battle of Chancellorsville took place a year earlier that soldiers encountered skeletons that had been buried in (too) shallow graves in 1863. Both armies sustained heavy casualties while Grant kept attempting to move the fighting to a setting more to his advantage. The heavy forest made coordinated movements almost impossible, and when Lee used Longstreet to counterattack on the second day, Longstreet was nearly killed by a shot to the neck, disabling him for the rest of the campaign. Finally, Grant's army disengaged and moved to the southeast, attempting to lure Lee into open-field fighting.

During the Battle of the Wilderness, Stuart's pushing of Confederate General Thomas L. Rosser's "Laurel Brigade" into a fight with the better-armed "Michigan Brigade" under General George Custer resulted in significant loss of life. And when Grant continued to maneuver his men toward Richmond, Lee continued to parry, with Stuart receiving some credit for success in delaying the advance of the Union forces.

The Battle of Yellow Tavern

In early May of 1864, Union cavalry commander Maj. General Philip Sheridan organized a massive raid against Confederate supply and railroad lines near Richmond. Moving aggressively, he crossed the North Anna River and seized Beaver Dam Station on the Virginia Central Railroad. Anticipating their arrival, the Confederate troops had already destroyed most of the critical military supplies, so Sheridan's men destroyed railroad cars, ripped out telegraph lines, and rescued several hundred (some estimates are in the thousands) Union captives.

On May 9, the largest cavalry force ever seen in the Eastern Theater, over 10,000 with 32 artillery pieces, arched southeast intending to slip behind Lee's army with three goals: to disrupt Lee's supply lines by destroying railroad tracks and supplies; to threaten the Confederate capital of Richmond; and most significantly for Sheridan, to take Stuart out of the war.

As expected, Stuart dispatched a force of about 3,000-4,500 cavalrymen to intercept Sheridan's cavalry. As Stuart rode to meet the enemy, accompanied by his aide, Maj. Andrew R. Venable, they stopped briefly to see Stuart's wife, Flora, and his children, Jimmie and Virginia. Venable later wrote, "He told me he never expected to live through the war, and that if we were conquered, that he did not want to live."[21]

At noon on May 11, 1864, the two forces met at Yellow Tavern, an abandoned inn six miles north of Richmond, Virginia. Not only did the Union outnumber the Confederates (ten to one by some estimates), it had superior firepower--armed with newly-developed rapid-firing Spencer carbine rifles.

After a spirited resistance by Confederate troops from the low ridge bordering the road to Richmond that lasted over three hours, the First Virginia Cavalry pushed the advancing Union soldiers back from the hilltop as Stuart, mounted on horseback in his conspicuous attire, rallied his men and encouraged them to keep pushing forward. While Union men of the Fifth Michigan Cavalry were steadily retreating, one of them, 48 year old sharpshooter John A. Huff, found himself only about 20 yards away from the vaunted and easily recognizable Stuart. Huff turned and shot Stuart with his .44-caliber pistol, sending a bullet slicing through his stomach and exiting his back, just right of his spine. In excruciating pain, an ambulance took Stuart to the home of his brother-in-law Dr. Charles Brewer, in Richmond, to await his wife's arrival.

The following day before Flora could reach his side, at 7:38 pm, Stuart died. In his final moments, Stuart ordered his sword and spurs be given to his son. His dying words were: "I am resigned; God's will be done."[22] He was just thirty-one years of age.

---

21   Wert, Jeffry D. *Cavalryman of the Lost Cause: A Biography of J.E.B. Stuart.* Page 349.
22   Wert, Jeffry D. *Cavalryman of the Lost Cause: A Biography of J.E.B. Stuart.* Pages 361- -362.

Stuart's grave

Chapter 8: Stuart's Legacy

The South Mourns

The death of Stuart brought a cloud of gloom to the South, said to be second only to that following the death of General "Stonewall" Jackson. Having known Stuart well before the war, Lee took the news of his death very hard, and witnesses observed him break down upon learning of Stuart's fate. Lee himself noted, "Among the gallant soldiers who have fallen in this war,

General Stuart was second to none in valor, in zeal, and in unfaltering devotion to his country. To military capacity of a high order and all the nobler virtues of the soldier he added the brighter graces of a pure life, guided and sustained by the Christian's faith and hope. The mysterious hand of an all-wise God has removed him from the scene of his usefulness and fame. His grateful countrymen will mourn his loss and cherish his memory. To his comrades in arms he has left the proud recollection of his deeds and his inspiring influence of his example."[23]

Following her husband's death, his wife Flora donned black mourning garb which she wore for the remaining 59 years of her life.

Stuart's Image

As a military man, few would dispute that "Jeb" Stuart was a born leader. He refined cavalry tactics (and even invented new ones as needed) and perfected the role of the cavalry as a reconnaissance and intelligence-gathering unit. And while content to play a supportive--even subordinate--role in battle, he repeatedly proved quite adept at taking charge and executing strategic moves fellow officers had not even considered. In fact, in all areas of military service, he garnered the highest of honors for his keen instincts, soldierly genius, and ever-readiness to step boldly into the fray. Stuart clearly attracted the notice of his opponents; Army of the Potomac Corps Commander John Sedgwick (who was also killed during the Overland Campaign) called Stuart, "the greatest cavalry officer ever foaled in America."

Still, he was a man of paradox who while not necessarily *misunderstood* in his lifetime, was seemingly never fully *known*.

Outwardly, Stuart was the embodiment of reckless courage, magnificent manhood, and unconquerable virility; a man who could wear--without drawing suspicion of instability--the flamboyant adornments of a classic cavalier. It was once written that his black plume and hat caught up with a golden star, seemed the proper frame for a knightly face. In that same vein, people were always aware that Stuart was engaging in public relations even then, and Civil War historian Jeff Wert captured it well: "Stuart had been the Confederacy's knight-errant, the bold and dashing cavalier, attired in a resplendent uniform, plumed hat, and cape. Amid a slaughterhouse, he had embodied chivalry, clinging to the pageantry of a long-gone warrior. He crafted the image carefully, and the image befitted him. He saw himself as the Southern people envisaged him. They needed a knight; he needed to be that knight." Stuart, in effect, was the very essence of the Lost Cause.

---

[23]   Lee, Robert E., Jr. *Recollections and Letters of General Robert E. Lee by Captain E. Lee, His Son.*

Yet inwardly, he was guarded about how his lighthearted, boyish silliness in camp might be misinterpreted; a laugh was always at his lips and a song behind it, and he would frequently lead an *impromptu* march with his banjo-player strumming at his side. As he rode down the lines at Chancellorsville, the commander of an army and successor to "Stonewall" Jackson, he is said to have sung a rollicking, "Old Joe Hooker, come out of the Wilderness."

Thus, he left it to those who really knew him to clarify that he never indulged in vices thought common to wartime soldiers (like drinking and tobacco), was never profane, and even abstained from card-playing. More importantly, perhaps, though frequently presented with opportunities for female companionship (something largely accepted in times of war for men far from home), he was a faithful husband and father, and said to be one of the purest of hearts the South ever produced.

Testament

Somewhat ironically, one of the first (and most enduring) accounts written about "Jeb" Stuart was not written by a Virginian--or even a Southerner--but by Johann August Heinrich Heros von Borcke (July 23, 1835--May 10, 1895), a German-American born of an aristocratic Prussian family who offered his services to the Confederate Army during the Civil War. A large, powerfully built and courageous man who joined Stuart's ranks in May of 1862, a mutual respect and admiration is said to have developed between the two men over the course of the two years they served together. Von Borcke was also present at some of the war's most noteworthy campaigns, including Stuart's famous ride around McClellan's army, the Battle of Fredericksburg, and the Battle of Yellow Tavern, where Stuart was mortally wounded. Von Borcke was nearly killed by a shot to the neck just before the Battle of Gettysburg, but he recovered to continue fighting in 1864 through the rest of the war.

Von Borcke

After being seriously wounded in battle while fighting at Stuart's side, von Borcke returned to Europe in December of 1864, and shortly after, began publishing his memoirs in *Blackwood's Magazine*; in 1866 he collected all his articles into *Memoirs of the Confederate Wars for Independence*. And in that von Borcke had no political agenda, was not a Southerner, and had no need to mythologize Stuart, this narrative is today viewed as one of the most objective accounts available of both Stuart and the war itself.

Echoing no Southern self-righteousness or support of the Confederacy's social or political grievances, *Memoirs* presents an insightful, humanized look into Stuart the man: a comrade; a friend; a dashing and daring cavalryman who "knew how to enjoy himself even in dangerous circumstances."[24] A man who, according to von Borcke, lacked any of the arrogance, mean-spirit, or self-centeredness associated with many of the Civil War's key figures, and who instilled lightheartedness in his men even in the most desperate of times.

As fate would have it, von Borcke died on May 10, 1895, 32 years to the day Stonewall Jackson died and nearly 31 years to the date of the Battle of Yellow Tavern, where Stuart was mortally wounded. Von Borcke died of complications from the grievous wound he suffered during the Battle of Middleburg in June 1863.

---

[24]   Escott, Paul D. "The Uses of Gallantry: Virginians and the Origins of J. E. B. Stuart's Historical Image." Page 1.

Similarly, in 1907, Union General Oliver O. Howard (who Stuart handily defeated at Chancellorsville) discussed Stuart in his autobiography, writing: "J. E. B. Stuart was cut out for a cavalry leader. In perfect health, but thirty-two years of age, full of vigor and enterprise, with the usual ideas imbibed in Virginia concerning State Supremacy, Christian in thought and temperate by habit, no man could ride faster, endure more hardships, make a livelier charge, or be more hearty and cheerful while so engaged. A touch of vanity, which invited the smiles and applause of the fair maidens of Virginia, but added to the zest and ardor of Stuart's parades and achievements. He commanded Lee's cavalry corps--a well-organized body, of which he was justly proud."[25]

Tribute

On May 30, 1907, a statue of "General J.E.B. Stuart" on horseback, sculpted by Frederick Moynihan, was dedicated on Richmond's famed Monument Avenue, at Stuart Circle. The fifteen foot statue has the horse's right foot raised and Stuart turned in his saddle facing east.

---

[25]   Howard, O. O. (Oliver Otis), *Autobiography of Oliver Otis Howard, Major General, United States Army.*

Stuart's Equestrian Statue in Richmond

In the 1940s, the U. S. Army named two World War II tanks, the M3 and M5, the "Stuart" tanks in his honor.

A high school in Falls Church, Virginia, is named the J.E.B. Stuart High School; the school's team nickname, "Raiders," honors his famous Civil War tactics.

In 1864, C. Nordendorf composed the song, "Southern Troopers Song," which is *"Dedicated to Genl J. E. B. Stuart and his gallant Soldiers."* (Sheet music, Danville, Virginia.)

Bibliography

Catton, Bruce. *This Hallowed Ground: The Story of the Union Side of the Civil War*. New York: Doubleday & Company, 1955.

Davis, Burke. *Jeb Stuart: The Last Cavalier*. New York: Random House, 1957.

Eaton, Clement. *Jefferson Davis*. New York: The Free Press, 1977.

Eicher, John H. & David, J. *Civil War High Commands*. Stanford: Stanford University Press, 2001.

Escott, Paul D. "The Uses of Gallantry: Virginians and the Origins of J. E. B. Stuart's Historical Image," *The Virginia Magazine of History and Biography*, Vol 103, No 1, 1995. Accessed via Jstor: http://www.jstor.org/discover/10.2307/4249485?uid=3739600&uid=2&uid=4&uid=3739256&sid=21100770232471 05.05.2012.

Garrison, Webb. *Civil War Curiosities*. Nashville: Rutledge Hill Press, 1994.

Howard, O. O. (Oliver Otis), *Autobiography of Oliver Otis Howard, Major General, United States Army*. New York: The Baker & Taylor Company, 1907. Accessed via http://archive.org/details/autobiographyofo01howarich 05.07.2012.

Lanning, Michael Lee. *The Civil War 100*. Illinois: Sourcebooks, Inc., 2006.

Lee, Robert E., Jr. *Recollections and Letters of General Robert E. Lee by Captain E. Lee, His Son*. Retrieved via http://www.quillspirit.org/ebooks/Letters_of_General_R_E_Lee/6.php 05.06.2012.

Mosby, John Singleton. *The Memoirs of Colonel John S. Mosby*. Boston: Little, Brown, and Company, 1917. Accessed via http://docsouth.unc.edu/fpn/mosby/menu.html 05.05.2012.

Philips, David. *Crucial Land Battles*. New York: MetroBooks, 1996.

Sears, Stephen W. *Chancellorsville*. Boston: Houghton Mifflin, 1996.
            Gettysburg. Boston: Houghton Mifflin, 2003.

Sifakis, Stewart, "Who Was Who In The Civil War." Accessed via: http://www.civilwarhome.com/stuartbi.htm 05.07.2012.

Stuart Family Archives: http://archiver.rootsweb.ancestry.com/th/read/STUART/2006-04/1144035927 Accessed 05.04.2012.

Stepp, John W. & Hill, William I. (editors), *Mirror of War, the Washington Star Reports the Civil War*. The Evening Star Newspaper Company, 1961.

Thomas, Emory M. *Bold Dragoon: The Life of J.E.B. Stuart*. Norman: University of Oklahoma Press, 1986.

Wert, Jeffry D. *Cavalryman of the Lost Cause: A Biography of J.E.B. Stuart*. New York: Simon & Schuster, 2008.

Wright, C. M. "Flora Cooke Stuart (1836–1923)." Retrieved via Encyclopedia Virginia: http://www.EncyclopediaVirginia.org/Stuart_Flora_Cooke_1836-1923 on 05.06.2012.

Nathan Bedford Forrest

Chapter 1: Forrest's Family Lineage

The Forrest Family

Of all the men who participated in the Civil War, Nathan Bedford Forrest has been universally acknowledged as one of the toughest and most courageous. To understand how Forrest became that man, a look at his childhood goes a long way toward providing an explanation.

Nathan Bedford Forrest was born near Chapel Hill, Bedford County, Tennessee on July 13, 1821, the first of 12 offspring to hardscrabble farmer-blacksmith William Forrest and his wife Miriam Beck. William Forrest's family had moved from Virginia to North Carolina, where various family members would fight in the Revolutionary War, and later to Tennessee during the second half of the 18th Century, while the Beck family moved from South Carolina to Tennessee a few years before them.

Heirs to English, Scottish, and Irish yeomen, the Forrests scraped by along the western frontier of America, trading in cattle, mules and horses for a century or so before the first of their family found prominence. Shadrack Forrest was identified in the 1800 North Carolina census as owning 780 acres of land and one slave. In 1806, Shadrack moved his family to Sumner County, Tennessee near Nashville, where they bought property.

In 1810, Shadrack's son, Nathan Forrest, bought 150 acres of land, and the following year, he and his father jointly purchased 470 more acres, making them substantial land owners. Eleven years later, in 1821, Miriam, the wife of Nathan's eldest son William, gave birth to Nathan

Bedford, apparently named after his grandfather and the county in which he was born. A recollection from a neighbor from that time describes the Forrest family as, "all energetic, high-minded, straightforward people. I have never heard of any of them being dissipated or connected with anything that was disreputable."[26]

The Beck Family

Of Scotch-Irish decent, the Becks emigrated to South Carolina sometime during the 1700s and then moved to Bedford County, Tennessee, where they acquired considerable land and were known to be a vigorous, tough-minded, and prolific family.

Surviving documents describe Nathan's mother, Miriam Beck, as a woman who stood five feet ten inches in height, weighed one hundred eighty pounds, had grey eyes, and was known to be so religious that she observed the Sabbath by cooking Sunday dinners on Saturday; a woman so stern and righteous that she once gave her son a serious thrashing with a peach-tree switch, even though he was 18 years old at the time.

In fact, vigorous might be selling Miriam short. After having 12 children by her husband William, she remarried after his death and produced four more.

Chapter 2: Early Life, 1821-1841

Childhood: 1821-1833

Born into poverty in the backwoods of Tennessee in 1821 and raised without formal education, Forrest and his family were "inured to hardship by seemingly endless labor," but that hard work would help Forrest establish himself as a prominent plantation owner and slave trader in the antebellum South.

By all accounts, Nathan's father could hardly be considered "accomplished" by any measure. The log cabin Nathan was born in belonged to the Beck family, William's work as a blacksmith seems to have been sporadic at best, and his father owned no land until six years after he and Miriam married, when in 1826 he somehow acquired 50 acres at a place called Spring Creek for a nominal fee of $1. A short time later, however, William sold those fifty acres for $400 which he applied to the purchase of 181 acres.

---

[26]   Hurst, Jack. *Nathan Bedford Forest, A Biography*. Page 19.

One of the factors thought to have shaped young Nathan's personality and worldview was the fact that he had survived when several of his sibling had not; two of his eight brothers and three of his sisters all died during childhood of typhoid fever. This in itself seems to have instilled in Nathan a particular passion for life that made him unlike other boys of his time and place.

The central factor, of course, was the frontier, and young Nathan was a frontier boy in every sense of the word. Known to many primarily by his various exploits and boyhood adventures, one often-told tale relates how Nathan single-handedly killed a large timber rattler while on a blackberry picking mission. Other stories tell how Nathan once dived repeatedly into a creek to recover a pocketknife for a friend, refusing to give up until he retrieved it; how when thrown from his horse into a pack of wild dogs he managed to frighten the dogs away, sending them howling into the woods; and of rushing a group of drunken loiterers with a pair of shears when they refused to vacate from in front of his uncle's tailor shop. Indeed, even before he'd reached his teens, Nathan showed signs of the indomitable traits and mastery of the backwoods he would later put fully on display as a general in the Confederate Army.

Teen Years: 1834-1840.

In 1834, Nathan's family gave up their plot in Spring Creek and moved to the "wilds" of Tippah County, Mississippi (now Benton County), where Nathan spent most of his youth helping out on the small hill farm his father leased from the Beck family (but never owned).

Although Nathan is said to have been an avid reader, he attended less than six months of formal school, and it's unlikely that even *subscription* schools, those paid for by the community, were established in what was still considered the "wilderness". Furthermore, after his father died in 1837, the 16 year old Forrest became head of the family as the eldest son.

Obliged to support his widowed mother and eleven siblings with no resources other than their meager plot of land, he devoted the next five years of his life to this work, neglecting his own education. As head of household, however, he did see to it that his brothers and sisters were provided as fine an education as was available in that place and time. He and his younger brothers cleared more land and continued the cultivation begun by their father, growing corn, wheat, oats, and cotton). Together the Forrests gradually increased their cattle, horses, and mules, eventually becoming one of the more prosperous families in the area.

Like Mother, Like Son

Another incident that speaks of the inimitable character that would come to define Nathan occurred in 1838, not long after his father's death.

On a return trip from welcoming a new neighbor, a trip requiring his mother and her sister Fanny to cover ten miles through the wilderness on horseback (for which they were rewarded a basket of chicks), within one mile of home they were attacked by a mountain lion which had apparently caught scent of the chicks. Though sustaining severe claw marks to her neck and shoulders, an attack which left their horse dead, Miriam refused to forfeit the basket of chicks. Afterwards, the bloodied women proceeded home on foot.

Immediately after dressing his mother's wounds, Nathan took a flintlock musket, rounded up the family's hounds, and disappeared into the night. By midnight, the dogs had the cat treed, but Nathan didn't have sufficient light to shoot the animal. Waiting at the foot of the tree until surrise, he killed the animal and by 9:00 a.m. retuned home carrying the cat's scalp and ears. After this event, Nathan had earned a fearless reputation within the area, with exploits American schoolchildren have come to associate with frontier icons like Daniel Boone and fellow Tennessean Davy Crockett.

Texas

By February 1841, the younger Forrest brothers - John, William, Aaron, Jesse, and Jeffery - were old enough to maintain the farm on their own so Nathan, now nearly 20 years of age, decided to enlist in a Mississippi volunteer army unit under Captain Wallace Wilson. This unit, and others like it across the South, intended to deal with Mexico's attempts to reclaim Texas, which had just years earlier won its independence and would not become a U.S. state for several more years.

Due to Wilson's poor management of the unit, however, it was forced to disband even before it set off for Texas, as a result of being unable to book steamer passage; the unit simply didn't have the money. But while most of the volunteers simply went home, Nathan paid his own way and finally arrived in the new settlement of Houston only to find his services unneeded. As it turned out, Mexico was making no advances, and it would be another five years before the Mexican-American War. Broke and disappointed, Nathan took a job splitting rails to obtain enough money to get back home.

Chapter 3: Personal Life, 1840-1861

A Man of *Questionable* Character

Little has been written about the childhood and early years of Nathan Bedford Forrest, in part because his lack of education made him incapable of writing well, and there is no indication he kept a journal. Thus, historians rely upon a few surviving accounts to piece together the picture of a man known primarily through his actions beginning at about the age of forty, at the start of the Civil War.

One very insightful and often-told anecdote illustrating Nathan's enigmatic character involves two stranded young ladies and two less-than-chivalrous young men the 24 year old Nathan encountered in 1845 along the road near his house. As the story goes, one late summer day Nathan came upon a black carriage driver struggling to free a coach stuck in a mud hole at a creek ford not far from his home near Hernando, Mississippi. Inside the coach were the widow Elizabeth Montgomery and her 18 year old daughter Mary Ann, two "proper" ladies who were new residents of the area.

As Nathan approached and assessed the scene, he saw that the two young men on horseback seemed perfectly willing to let the slave struggle on his own to free the carriage, apparently offering no assistance whatsoever. Pulling to one side of the road, Nathan hitched his horse to a fence and waded out to the carriage through the mud, introduced himself, and obtained the women's permission to carry them one at a time to dry ground. Afterwards, he waded back into the mud to help the unfortunate driver free the now-lightened coach.

As he lifted the two women back into the coach, Nathan harshly chastised the two young men for their uselessness, and then proceeded to threaten them with physical harm if they didn't leave immediately, which they did. With what would later be recognized as typical Forrest boldness, just before the ladies pulled away, Nathan asked permission to formally call upon them at their home. In light of the chivalry he'd shown, they consented.

While this had been the first time the two women had met Nathan, considering the notoriety that already surrounded the brash and often volatile young man, it seems likely they had at least *heard* of him prior to that encounter; perhaps even read about him in the local newspapers. In a front page story appearing in the Memphis-based *American Eagle* a few months earlier, it was reported that in what was termed a "most bloody affray," Nathan had apparently intervened on his uncle's behalf (one Jonathan Forrest) when the Matlock brothers shot his uncle during a business deal gone awry.[27] As the story was reported, Nathan stepped forward, drew his two-shot pistol and shot the younger Matlock (known as T. J.) through the shoulder, and then fired on the elder Matlock, shooting him through the arm (which later had to be amputated). Then when the other two Matlock brothers lit upon him, he took a knife tossed to him by someone in the crowd and proceeded to stab them mercilessly. Nathan was also wounded in the encounter. Incredibly, one of the Matlock brothers would serve under Forrest during the Civil War.

---

[27]   Hurst, Jack. *Nathan Bedford Forest, A Biography*. Page 16.

Local legend says this was not the first or last time Nathan was involved in such an incident, and obituaries would later note, "He was known to his acquaintances as a man of obscure origin and low associations, a shrewd speculator, negro trader, and duelist, but a man of great energy and brute courage."

Marriage

Just prior to the Civil War, Nathan Bedford Forrest was known to many as a Memphis speculator and Mississippi gambler, and his volatility had a penchant for getting him in duels. But when he came calling on the Montgomery ladies in the summer of 1845, he presented himself as a young, successful mercantile dealer with an office on the public square of their mutual county, DeSoto.

As he approached the Montgomery home, Nathan found the two "useless" young men he'd met that day on the muddy road sitting on the front porch. Upon recognizing that they too were prospective suitors, he immediately handed them their hats (despite one being a minister) and ordered them to leave the premises, which they quickly obliged. Once invited inside, Nathan wasted no time in proposing to Mary Ann, presenting his case succinctly as to why he would make the ideal husband: he cleverly argued that if Mary Ann were to accept as a suitor one of the two boys he'd so tactfully dismissed, she could expect to frequently find herself as helpless as she did that day at the creek, whereas, he and his profitable business could support her securely and comfortably. She told him she would have to consider it.

Upon his second visit, Nathan arrived with marriage license in hand, assuring her that he intended to marry her; and on his third, she finally accepted. On September 25, 1845, the two were married, but if Mary Anne's uncle and guardian, the Reverend Samuel Montgomery Cowan had gotten his way, the wedding would never have taken place. According to a classmate of Mary Ann who happened to be visiting the Montgomerys, when Nathan approached the Reverend Montgomery Cowen for his blessing (and to officiate the ceremony), the reverend is said to have stated emphatically, "Why, Bedford, I could never consent! You cuss and gamble, and Mary Ann is a good Christian girl." To this the clever Nathan countered, "I know that, reverend! And that's just why I want her!"[28]

The newlywed Forrests set up housekeeping in a relatively simple Hernando home constructed of two log cabins built side-by-side, then covered with clapboards to form a single house. As far as lodgings went, it was above average for the Southwest frontier, but hardly what Mary Ann expected from such a *successful* entrepreneur. What Nathan had neglected to tell Mary Ann was that the death of his uncle Jonathan, who had been his partner in many business dealings, had left

---

[28]   Hurst, Jack. *Nathan Bedford Forest, A Biography*. Page 17.

him in considerable debt. In fact, although he owned a home, five slaves, five horses, twenty head of cattle, fifteen sheep, two oxen, a wagon, and seventy-five barrels of corn, he was tens of thousands of dollars in debt. This would, of course, change considerably over the course of the next 15 years, but that would have been no comfort to Mary Ann at the time. The Forrests would have at least two children: William Montgomery Bedford, born in 1845, and a daughter, Fanny, who died when she was five years old.

Over the course of the next two decades, Forrest was extremely active in several endeavors. He captained a boat which ran between Memphis, Tennessee and Vicksburg, Mississippi, he profitably engaged in plantation speculation, and he became the nominal owner of two plantations not far from Goodrich's Landing near Vicksburg, where he had 100 or more slaves toiling for him. Given his status as a prominent slaveowner and trader, acclaimed writer Shelby Foote would later try to soften contemporary criticism of Forrest's slavetrading by noting he "avoided splitting up families or selling to cruel plantation owners."

Regardless, by the time the Civil War broke out, Forrest had made himself one of the richest men in the South.

FORREST & MAPLES,

SLAVE DEALERS,

87 Adams Street,
Between Second and Third,

MEMPHIS, TENNESSEE,

Have constantly on hand the best selected assortment of

FIELD HANDS, HOUSE SERVANTS & MECHANICS,

at their Negro Mart, to be found in the city. They are daily receiving from Virginia, Kentucky and Missouri, fresh supplies of likely Young Negroes.

Negroes Sold on Commission,

and the highest market price always paid for good stock. Their Jail is capable of containing Three Hundred, and for comfort, neatness and safety, is the best arranged of any in the Union. Persons wishing to purchase, are invited to examine their stock before purchasing elsewhere.

They have on hand at present, Fifty likely young Negroes, comprising Field hands, Mechanics, House and Body Servants, &c.

Chapter 4: The Civil War, 1861-1865

Unlikely Soldier

By the time the Civil War started in 1861, Nathan Bedford Forrest was one of the richest men in the South, with income from cotton, livestock, real estate, and slaves accruing a personal fortune estimated at $1.5 million. Although major planters were exempt from military service, when Nathan heard that his native Tennessee had voted to secede from the Union and join the

Confederacy, he couldn't wait to volunteer. On July 14, 1861, Nathan, along with his youngest brother Jeffery and fifteen-year-old son William, enlisted as a private, joining Captain Josiah White's Company "E" Tennessee Mounted Rifles. His superior officers, as well as Tennessee state governor Isham G. Harris, were surprised to find someone of Forrest's wealth and prominence amongst the ranks.

Forrest may have been a common soldier but for the fact that local officials wished to utilize his wealth and status. In October 1861, Governor Harris authorized Nathan to raise and fund his own cavalry regiment, which he quickly accomplished by posting ads inviting "men with good horse and good gun" to join his regiment "if you wanna have some fun and to kill some Yankees.")[29]

Impressed with his natural leadership and ability to train men (despite having no training himself), the governor commissioned him Lieutenant Colonel Nathan Bedford Forest and directed him to prepare his troops for action. It also helped that Forrest was a commanding 6'2, 210 pounds, truly the "most man", as Shelby Foote later put it.

From the beginning of the war, Forrest displayed quick and sound judgment, with a gift for executing tactics that often succeeded due to their sheer boldness. With his own unit, known as "Forrest's Cavalry Corps", he immediately organized a raid to confiscate Union equipment, and he even took two Union sympathizers hostage, hoping to exchange them for two Southern compatriots the Union was holding.

Fort Donelson

Despite the loss of Fort Sumter in April 1861, the North expected a relatively quick victory, and their expectations weren't unrealistic, given the Union's overwhelming economic advantages over the South. At the start of the war, the Union had a population of over 22 million. The South had a population of 9 million, nearly 4 million of whom were slaves. Union states contained 90% of the manufacturing capacity of the country and 97% of the weapon manufacturing capacity. Union states also possessed over 70% of the total railroads in the pre-war United States at the start of the war, and the Union also controlled 80% of the shipbuilding capacity of the pre-war United States.

But while the Lincoln Administration and most Northerners were preoccupied with trying to capture Richmond in the summer of 1861, the most decisive actions early in the Civil War took place in the Western theater. At the beginning of the fighting, Confederate forces had occupied both Fort Henry on the Tennessee River and Fort Donelson on the Cumberland River in

---

[29]   Burns, Ken (director, PBS). *The Civil War, Episode 7,* "Most Hallowed Ground."

Tennessee, affording them strategic control of Western Kentucky and the primary water routes from the Ohio River into Tennessee. At the time, both sides were hoping border states like Kentucky that had not yet picked a side would join theirs. Lincoln himself famously quipped, "I hope to have God on my side, but I must have Kentucky."

In January 1862, an unheralded general in command of the District of Southeast Missouri persuaded his superior to allow him to launch a campaign on the Tennessee River. At the time, Ulysses S. Grant owed his position more to politics than any demonstrable military skill, but he would prove to be the North's greatest general, beginning with this campaign. As soon as his superior, General Henry "Old Brains" Halleck acquiesced, Grant moved against Fort Henry, in close coordination with the naval command of Flag Officer Andrew Hull Foote. The tag team of infantry and naval bombardment helped force the capitulation of Fort Henry on February 6, 1862.

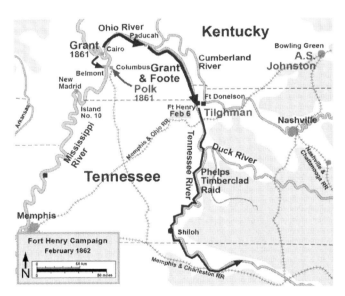

On February 14, Lieutenant Colonel Forrest's cavalry unit was attached to the Confederate garrison manning Fort Donelson, a strategically important position. After forcing the surrender of Fort Henry, Grant and Foote immediately followed it up with an attack on Fort Donelson on the Cumberland River, which earned Grant his famous nickname "Unconditional Surrender". With the help of the naval forces, Grant's soldiers enveloped the Confederate garrison at Fort Donelson, which included Confederate generals Simon Buckner, John Floyd, and Gideon Pillow. In one of the most bungled operations of the war, the Confederate generals tried and failed to open an escape route by attacking Grant's forces on February 15. During the fighting, Forrest's men captured a Union battery, and although the initial assault was successful, General Pillow inexplicably chose to have his men pull back into their trenches, ostensibly so they could grab more supplies before their escape. Instead, they simply lost all the ground they had taken, and the garrison was cut off yet again.

During the early morning hours of February 16, the garrison's generals held one of the Civil War's most famous councils of war. The three generals agreed to surrender their army, but none of them wanted to be the fall guy, so Floyd, Pillow, and Buckner bickered among themselves as to who would officiate the surrender, and who would be allowed to execute a timely escape. With an unmistakable and comically inflated sense of self-importance, General Floyd (who had a history of retreating from battles and feared he'd be executed if captured) relinquished command to Pillow (who thought he served the greatest loss to the Confederacy if captured), who then relinquished command to Buckner, the least senior officer. At that council, Forrest strongly protested the plan to surrender the garrison and insisted everyone could escape. But Forrest was still only a no-name cavalry officer, and he was dealing with some of the Confederacy's most vainglorious leaders.

Upon conveying their intentions to Forrest, Pillow immediately crossed the Cumberland in a skiff, while Floyd prepared to escape with his two regiments (about two thousand men) via two approaching steamers. At the boat landing, Floyd ordered the men of the 20th Mississippi to form a barricade to prevent the remainder of the fort's garrison from deserting while he and his men boarded and escaped across the Cumberland to Nashville. Realizing that like Buckner's eleven thousand men, his men were to be sacrificed, Forrest refused to make it so easy for the enemy.

With no attempt to conceal his anger at the cowardice displayed by his commanding officers, Forrest announced, "I did not come here to surrender my command!"[30] He then proceeded to round up his own men and rallied nearly 4,000 total before leading them on a daring and dramatic escape under the cover of darkness through the icy waters of Lick Creek to escape the siege and avoid capture. Ultimately, this spawned a loyalty from his men that few Confederate leaders enjoyed; becoming the first notch in the belt for the general who would come to be known as "The Wizard of the Saddle."

Despite all of these successful escapes, General Buckner still decided to surrender to Grant. As a long-standing legend describes, when asked for terms of surrender, Grant sent a letter stating, "No terms except an unconditional and immediate surrender." [31]

---

[30]   Gott, Kendall D. *Where the South Lost the War: An Analysis of the Fort Henry—Fort Donelson Campaign.* Pages 240-241.
[31]   Grant, U. S. (John. Y. Simon, editor). *Ulysses S. Grant: Memoirs and Selected Letters.*

Floyd

Buckner

Pillow

Grant's campaign was the first major success for Union forces in the war, which had already lost the disastrous First Battle of Bull Run in July 1861 and was reorganizing the Army of the Potomac in anticipation of the Peninsula Campaign, which would fail in the summer of 1862. The capture of Fort Donelson by the Union army accomplished several significant objectives: it ensured that Kentucky would remain in the Union, set the stage for the invasion (and subsequent occupation) of Tennessee, secured the Tennessee and Cumberland Rivers for Union Army transportation of troops and supplies, and led to the eventual control of the Mississippi River, initially recognized by Union war planners like Winfield Scott as the key to winning a protracted war.

Fort Donelson also elevated Ulysses S. Grant from an obscure and largely unproven leader to the rank of major general, while both the Union and Confederacy got their first real taste of Forrest's tenacity. It wouldn't take long for Forrest to display it again.

The Battle of Shiloh

A replica of Shiloh Church. The original was ruined during the battle.

Grant had just secured Union command of precious control over much of the Mississippi River and much of Kentucky and Tennessee, but that would prove to be merely a prelude to the Battle of Shiloh, which at the time was the biggest battle ever fought on the continent.

After the victories at Fort Henry and Fort Donelson, Grant was now at the head of the Army of the Tennessee, which was nearly 50,000 strong and firmly encamped at Pittsburg Landing on the western side of the Tennessee River. The losses had dismayed the Confederates, who quickly launched an offensive in an attempt to wrest control of Tennessee from the Union.

At the head of the Confederate army was Albert Sidney Johnston, President Jefferson Davis's favorite general, and widely considered the South's best general. On the morning of April 6, Johnston directed an all out attack on Grant's army around Shiloh Church, and though Grant's men had been encamped there, they had failed to create defensive fortifications or earthworks. They were also badly caught by surprise. With nearly 45,000 Confederates attacking, Johnston's army began to steadily push Grant's men back toward the river.

As fate would have it, the Confederates may have been undone by friendly fire at Shiloh. Johnston advanced out ahead of his men on horseback while directing a charge near a peach orchard when he was hit in the lower leg by a bullet that historians now widely believe was fired by his own men. Nobody thought the wound was serious, including Johnston, who continued to aggressively lead his men and even sent his personal physician to treat wounded Union soldiers taken captive. But the bullet had hit an artery, and Johnston began to feel faint in the saddle. With blood filling up his boot, Johnston unwittingly bled to death.

Johnston

Johnston's death was hidden from his men, and command fell upon P.G.T. Beauregard, who was the South's hero at Fort Sumter and at the First Battle of Bull Run. General Beauregard was competent, but Johnston's death naturally caused a delay in the Confederate command. It was precious time that Grant and General Sherman used to rally their troops into a tight defensive position around Pittsburg Landing.

That night, nearly 20,000 soldiers from Don Carlos Buell's Army of the Ohio began streaming in under the cover of darkness to back up Grant, but their arrival was noticed by Colonel Forrest's well-placed scouts. Forrest attempted to take the news to General Beauregard, but Beauregard was nowhere to be found. With Forrest unable to rouse and sufficiently organize the troops himself, when Grant attacked at dawn with his army now totaling nearly sixty thousand men, the South's thirty-five thousand battle-worn soldiers simply couldn't withstand the onslaught.

The following morning, Grant's army, now reinforced by Don Carlos Buell's 20,000 strong Army of the Ohio, launched a successful counterattack that drove the Confederates off the field and back to Corinth, Mississippi. And Forrest was in the thick of it. Forrest was instrumental in protecting the Confederate rear guard with his cavalry, securing their retreat south. Grant's army had just won the biggest battle in the history of North America, with nearly 24,000 combined casualties among the Union and Confederate forces.

The following day, April 8, Forrest nearly changed the course of history. After the victory at Shiloh, Grant ordered Sherman to advance some men south down the road to Corinth to determine whether the Confederates were regrouping or retreating. As they did so, Sherman came upon a Confederate field hospital, which was fiercely protected when Forrest ordered a bold cavalry charge. The skirmish, known as the Battle of Fallen Timbers, nearly resulted in Forrest's 300 cavalry chargers capturing Sherman himself, and Forrest led from the front, to the extent that he got out ahead of his own men and began shooting and using his saber before realizing he was alone and surrounded by Union troops, one of whom cried out, "Kill that goddamn Rebel! Knock him off his horse!"[32] In the melee, a nearby Union soldier put his musket to Forrest's side and fired, nearly blowing him out of his saddle. Incredibly, Forrest continued to fight, grabbing a Union soldier and pulling him into the saddle to use him as a human shield. Forrest spun his horse around and galloped off bleeding, making his escape despite having a bullet lodged near his spine. A week later, it would be removed without the benefit of anesthesia.

By now, it was becoming clear to the Union that Forrest was competent in conducting traditional cavalry roles like reconnaissance and screening an army, and he was a "devil" while fighting. Sherman himself would later label Forrest "the most remarkable man our Civil War produced on either side." One of Grant's friends noted Forrest "was the only Confederate cavalryman of whom Grant stood in much dread."

Sherman

[32]   Gaffney, P. and D. Gaffney. *The Civil War: Exploring History One Week at a Time.* Page 103.

Brigadier General Forrest

With Union armies now occupying middle Tennessee, Colonel Forrest executed a series of brilliant cavalry maneuvers within that territory that quickly made his name known across America and earned him promotion to Brigadier General on July 21, 1862. His crack cavalry brigade then hung onto Union general Buell's flank during his march into Kentucky, protected General Bragg's retreat from Tullahoma to the Tennessee River, and that winter, while the army was in winter quarters, vigorously covered the Union front at Nashville, continually stinging the enemy at every opportunity.

By December of 1862, Union forces were amassing two huge, independent armies. On the Mississippi, General Ulysses S. Grant was preparing to threaten Vicksburg, while at Nashville, Maj. General William Rosecrans' Army of the Cumberland was setting-up to drive southward toward Chattanooga. And with neither commander appearing to be willing to wait until spring to initiate their offensives, a Confederate winter strategy was urgently needed.

Confederate President Jefferson Davis sat in on closed-door discussions as Western Theater commander General Braxton Bragg decided that General Forrest would establish operations in west Tennessee to frustrate Grant, while Brig. General John Hunt Morgan and his Army of Tennessee would sweep north around Rosecrans' base at Nashville and attempt to sever Union supply lines by destroying key railroads and bridges in Kentucky. For his part, Forrest and his men had already destroyed nearly sixty miles of train track, greatly frustrating Grant. This set the stage for Forrest to play a critical role in numerous cavalry operations, his primary mission to torment Union forces by striking at their most vulnerable points.

In December 1862 and again in January 1863, Forrest led a raid into west Tennessee which ultimately contributed to Grant's abandonment of his initial campaign in central Mississippi. Then in February, Forrest and General Joseph Wheeler attacked Fort Donelson in a skirmish known as the Battle of Dover but were readily repelled by the relatively small Union garrison, which Forrest blamed on Wheeler. Infuriated, Forrest told him in no uncertain terms, "Tell [General Bragg] that I will be in my coffin before I will fight again under your command!"[33]

In early 1863 Forrest was ordered to conduct extensive raids in an effort to sever the communication lines of Union General William Rosecrans' Army of the Cumberland, Forrest entered Tennessee with less than one thousand men and managed to capture McMinnville. He then took the Union garrison of 2,000 men at Murfreesboro by surprise, capturing all the survivors, including Union Major General Thomas L. Crittenden. The quick moving Forrest proved impossible to trap for the Union, and by the time he finished his series of raids, he

---

[33]   Bearss, Edwin C. (William C. Davis and Julie Hoffman, editors). "Joseph Wheeler," In *The Confederate General.* Page 126.

actually returned to Mississippi with more men under his command than he started with.

One of Forrest's greatest accomplishments came at the end of April. On April 30, Forrest confronted cavalry led by Union General Able Streight, who had launched a cavalry raid from Rome, Georgia that became known as "Streight's Raid". Forrest harassed Streight's troopers at Sand Mountain throughout April, and in May he tricked Streight into thinking he had a larger force by making his men parade in plain sight of the enemy, giving the impression he had many more men than he actually had. When Streight surrendered his nearly 3,000 strong force, it turned out he had so many more men than Forrest that that Forrest had to enlist local civilians to guard them.

Chickamauga and the Year of the Feud

In the summer of 1863, Forrest was again assigned by General Braxton Bragg to serve under General Joseph Wheeler. Considering their history, Forrest demanded that he be transferred to west Tennessee, and was subsequently dispatched there with a pitifully small force (perhaps as a form of reprimand). Not to be deterred, Forrest recruited additional men from the area and soon had a force large enough to give Union commanders ongoing headaches.

On September 19-20, 1863, the Confederate Army of Tennessee under Braxton Bragg decisively defeated General Rosecrans' Army of the Cumberland at the Battle of Chickamauga. Rosecrans committed a blunder by exposing a gap in part of his line that General James Longstreet drove through, sending Rosecrans and nearly 20,000 of his men into a disorderly retreat. Forrest commanded the cavalry of the right wing, and he led a charge during the battle that picked up hundreds of retreating Union stragglers. The destruction of the Union army was prevented only by General George H. Thomas, who rallied the remaining parts of the army and formed a defensive stand on Horseshoe Ridge. Dubbed "The Rock of Chickamauga", Thomas's heroics ensured that Rosecrans' army was able to successfully retreat back to Chattanooga.

Still, the Confederates had a great chance to strike a fatal blow to Rosecrans' army, and Bragg was strongly urged by some of his subordinates, including Forrest and General James Longstreet, to follow up the success at Chickamauga with a decisive advance on Chattanooga. Bragg's failure to do so left both Forrest and Longstreet incredulous. Longstreet would constantly feud with Bragg over the next few months, while Forrest openly asked, "What does he fight battles for?" In one of the most famous confrontations of the Civil War, Forrest threatened Bragg's life during a heated exchange, telling his commanding officer, "I have stood your meanness as long as I intend to! You have played the part of the scoundrel, and are a coward! If you were any part of a man, I would slap your jowls and force you to resent it! You may as well not issue orders to me, for I will not obey them! And I say to you that if you ever again try to interfere with me or cross my path, it will be at the peril of your life!"[34]

Forrest was so dissatisfied with the incompleteness of the victory and ineptness of his superiors that he tendered his resignation from the army. Of course, no matter how often he feuded with other generals, the Confederacy realized he was indispensable. As the commanding officer, Bragg used his power to remove Longstreet from his presence by giving him an independent command, and Bragg gave Forrest an independent command in Mississippi.

Despite these arguments, by the end of 1863 Forrest had earned himself accolades for his strategy, tactics, courage, and fighting, earning a promotion to major general. But it was also apparent that his volatile temperament hurt his relationship with fellow officers, especially those he deemed incompetent. Ironically, he almost never had the chance to feud with Bragg because he was convalescing in the run up to the Battle of Chickamauga as a result of an infamous encounter earlier that month. In early September, Forrest famously feuded with Lieutenant Andrew Wills Gould, an artillery officer under his command, after an ambush during Streight's Raid that resulted in Forrest's men losing two cannons. Forrest accused Gould of cowardice for the loss of the guns and attempted to transfer Gould, leading the young headstrong officer to confront Forrest personally. The confrontation got more heated, when Gould allegedly shouted, "No man can accuse me of cowardice and both of us live!" As Forrest reached for a penknife, Gould reached for his gun, and in the scramble Forrest was shot in the abdomen. Somehow, the injured Forrest managed to subdue Gould and stabbed him, causing a severe wound.

Incredibly, the fight was still not over. Gould rushed out of the room gushing blood, and he was quickly taken to a field hospital. Meanwhile, Forrest thought he had been mortally wounded and became blind with rage, shouting, "Get out of my way! I am mortally wounded and will kill the man who has shot me!" Forrest grabbed pistols and headed to the hospital to finish off Gould, but Gould made a mad dash out of the hospital when he saw Forrest coming. When Forrest fired a shot at Gould, it ricocheted off a wall and struck another soldier in the leg. Gould didn't get far before fainting, which pleased Forrest, who reportedly stuck him with his boot. Forrest would later learn to his great surprise that his wound was not serious, and Gould would die a few weeks later of his wound.

Fort Pillow

Forrest was proving to be a pain to some powerful Confederate generals, but the South was acutely aware that Forrest was an even bigger pain to the North. At the end of 1863, Forrest began operations in west Tennessee with a small unit, but he managed to recruit several thousand volunteers, including a number of veteran soldiers, and he whipped them into shape so that they were combat ready before their first confrontation. Upon hearing of Forrest's growing aptitude for adaptive warfare, General Sherman wrote to Union Commander-in-Chief Henry Halleck that

---

34   Wright, Mike. *What They Didn't Teach You About the Civil War*. Page 222.

men like Forrest are "men that must all be killed or employed by us before we can hope for peace. They have no property or future, and therefore cannot be influenced by anything except personal considerations."[35] Sherman repeatedly ordered his Memphis commanders to catch "that devil Forrest", essentially putting a bounty on his head.

Forrest already had a controversial Civil War record entering 1864, but he was about to participate in perhaps the most controversial battle of the war. After functioning as an independent raider for the next several months, on April 12, 1864, units of Forrest's cavalry surrounded Fort Pillow on the Mississippi River, north of Memphis. Ironically, the fort had been built in 1861 and named after General Gideon Pillow, the same General Pillow who proved wildly incompetent at Fort Donelson and ignored Forrest's suggestion to escape the siege instead of surrendering to Grant.

As far as skirmishes go, Fort Pillow was a completely unremarkable fight. Before attacking, Forrest demanded the unconditional surrender of the Union garrison, a normal custom of his, and he warned the Union commanding officer that he would not be responsible for his soldiers' actions if the warning went unheeded. What made Fort Pillow markedly different was that a sizable amount of the Union garrison defending the Fort was comprised of black soldiers, which particularly enraged Confederate soldiers whenever they encountered those they viewed as former slaves in the field.

It is still unclear exactly how the fighting unfolded, but what is clear is that an unusually high percentage of Union soldiers were killed, and the Confederates were accused of massacring black soldiers after they had surrendered. Primary sources tell conflicting accounts of what happened at Battle of Fort Pillow, leaving scholars to piece together the battle and determine whether Confederate soldiers purposely shot Union soldiers after they had surrendered..

---

[35] Sherman, W. T. (Charles Royster, notes). *Memoirs of General William T. Sherman*, Vol. I. Page 363.

News of the "Fort Pillow Massacre" quickly spread across the country, and it enraged the North. Black soldiers across the country began wearing patches that simply read, "Remember Fort Pillow", and the outrage was instrumental in forcing the Union to threaten to execute Confederate prisoners of war if the Union's black soldiers were not treated properly when captured themselves. Arguments over whether a massacre actually occurred, and what role Forrest played in it, continue to this day. Recent Forrest biographer Brian Steel Wills, taking his subject's past into account, labeled evidence of Forrest's participation in a massacre at Fort Pillow "circumstantial or questionable," claiming Forrest's war record "does not substantiate this charge." Fort Pillow historian Richard Fuchs charges Forrest with full complicity in the massacre, arguing that pro-Forrest arguments appear "designed to prevent any distraction from the hero worship" of Forrest. Author Shelby Foote credited Forrest for "doing all he could to end" the slaughter, while author Robert Browning Jr. argued that since Forrest "lost control of his men," he "shoulders the responsibility for the unnecessary deaths."

While General Forrest conceded that unarmed Blacks were indeed killed, he would not specify whether this had taken place during or after the battle, either upon his orders or from one of his field commanders. All Forrest confirmed in his report was that "the river was dyed with blood of the slaughtered troops for two hundred yards."[36] Forrest also noted in the report, "The approximate loss was upward of five hundred killed, but few of the officers escaping. My loss was about twenty killed. It is hoped that these facts will demonstrate to the Northern people that negro soldiers cannot cope with Southerners."

By May 1864, the Fort Pillow affair became a matter of congressional enquiry, with many leaders from both Union and Confederate camps anxious to condemn Forrest simply on principle alone. Certainly those who had personally experienced his temper and knew of his volatile reputation could easily imagine him capable of a massacre. Somewhat surprisingly, one of the men who believed Forrest was not guilty of an intentional massacre was General Sherman, who by 1864 begrudgingly admired his troublesome adversary. Based on statements taken from many of his own men who had been taken prisoner by Forrest and attested that "he was usually very kind to them," Sherman stated, "No doubt Forrest's men acted like a set of barbarians, shooting down the helpless negro garrison after the fort was in their possession; but I am told that Forrest personally disclaims any active participation in the assault. I also take it for granted that Forrest did not lead the assault in person, and consequently that he was to the rear, out of sight if not of hearing at the time."[37]

Regardless, Fort Pillow permanently marred Forrest's reputation for the rest of his life, and it was featured prominently in his obituaries throughout the North in 1877.

---

[36]   Lanning, Michael. *The Civil War 100*. Page 83.
[37]   Sherman, W. T. (Charles Royster, notes). *Memoirs of General William T. Sherman*, Vol. II. Page 470.

The Battle of Brice's Cross Roads

By late spring of 1864, General Sherman was preparing his armies for an invasion of Georgia that came to be known as the Atlanta Campaign. Combined, Sherman's armies formed the biggest army in American history, and Sherman set his sights on the Confederacy's last major industrial city in the West and the General Joseph E. Johnston's Army of Tennessee, which aimed to protect it. Johnston was hopelessly outnumbered, and he would spend much of the summer retreating closer and closer to Atlanta, but in the meantime, the Confederates recognized Napoleon's famous maxim that an army marches on its stomach. To lead such a gigantic force, Sherman needed to have secure supply lines and communication lines, relying heavily on railroads. Major General Forrest understood this as well, and he fully exploited it, resulting in his greatest victory.

On June 1, Forrest led his men from their supply base at Tupelo, Mississippi, intending to raid Sherman's railroad supply line in Tennessee. As fate would have it, however, on that very same day, Union Maj. General Samuel D. Sturgis marched out of Union headquarters near Memphis with about 8,000 men headed for Tupelo in search of Forrest. Following several days of miserable weather that brought troops and artillery movement to a virtual crawl, on June 7, Sturgis called a staff meeting to discuss the possibility of a new strategy; possibly going back to base and choosing an alternate approach. Under his command were cavalry commander Brig. General Benjamin H. Grierson, infantry commander Colonel William L. McMillen, and 93rd Indiana Infantry commander Colonel De Witt Thomas. Colonel McMillen convinced Sturgis to continue on rather than turn back in disgrace.

Unbeknownst to Sturgis, Confederate intelligence reports had alerted Confederate leaders of Sturgis' movement, and Forrest was sent to intercept his men. However, even though Forrest knew precisely where Sturgis would be (by June 9, the Union column would reach Brice's Cross Roads), he didn't have enough men to mount an offensive alone, so he set out to beef-up his cavalry with men gleaned from various scattered army camps along the Mobil & Ohio Railroad, planning to meet up with the enemy at the crossroads with more intimidating numbers.

Ultimately mustering three mounted units under Colonel W. A. Johnson and H. B. Lyon, Colonel Edmund Rucker, and Colonel Tyree Bell, Forrest's strategy was to obliterate Sturgis' cavalry which, by his estimation, would reach the crossroads three hours before his infantry. As he told Colonel Rucker that morning, "[Brice's Cross Roads] is densely wooded and the undergrowth so heavy that when we strike them they won't know how few men we have. In this heat, and coming on at a run five or six miles over muddy road, their infantry will be so tired we will ride right over them!"[38]

The next day, June 10, Forrest's 4,800 men engaged Sturgis' 8,000, with Forrest successfully executing some of the most brilliant military tactics used in the Civil War. Utilizing horses to move his men quickly from one point to another, he instructed them to dismount and concentrate their firepower at key positions--then remount and move the action to another location; stinging, moving, and stinging again. At times during the fighting, fierce hand-to-hand combat ensued, with the struggle so close at some points that weapons couldn't be reloaded and were instead used as clubs.

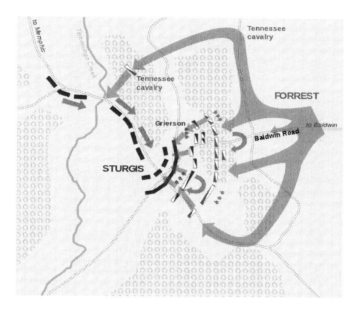

So fast and furious was Forrest's all-out assault that General Grierson became convinced he was facing far superior numbers, and finally requested that he be allowed to withdraw his entire cavalry. Union commander Colonel De Witt Thomas recorded this incident, writing, "One of the hardest battles I have ever witnessed! The enemy flanking me every few moments and my men charging their front, contesting for every foot of ground . . . I pressed again upon the enemy . . . was again outflanked and had to again give back, which I did by retreating and firing . . . ."[39]

About 4:00 that afternoon, Forrest was seen racing up and down the front line on horseback,

[38]   Brown, Dee. (Stan Banash, editor). *Dee Brown's Civil War Anthology*. Page 193.
[39]   Brown, Dee. (Stan Banash, editor). *Dee Brown's Civil War Anthology*. Page 198.

shouting encouragement to his men, just prior to ordering another charge along the line and doubling-up of troops at the Union crossroads position. At his signal, the Confederates then began a furious barrage of small arms and artillery that stunned Union officers who were convinced that Forrest's artillery was heavily supported by a line of riflemen, which they were not.

Sending the 59th Colored Regiment to hold off the Confederates with bayonets and muskets for clubbing, the Union troops initiated retreat, leaving confusion and pandemonium in their wake. It was reported that some of the black soldiers discarded their "Remember Fort Pillow" badges, worried that Confederate soldiers spotting them would kill them or treat them more harshly, and after the battle, Union leaders again accused Forrest of massacring unarmed and helpless black soldiers. Whether that was true or not, the extent of the damage to Sturgis's force was clear to everyone, including the general himself. In his official report, Sturgis wrote, "The enemy pressed heavily on the rear, so there was nothing left but to keep in motion. The artillery and train have already gone to hell! My soldiers are nothing but a mob!"[40]

That night in the darkness, the retreating Union column took the wrong road across Hatchie Swamp, resulting in wagons, artillery, and ambulances sinking into the deep mud. Sturgis was resigned to simply abandon them where they stood. When Forrest reached the swamp at 3:00 a.m., he found dozens of drowned and dying horses and mules, a mile-long caravan of burning wagons, numerous cannon and other artillery, and a row of abandoned ambulances filled with wounded men begging for medical attention, all buried in the bog.

As Forrest sent his men to continue the harassment of the retreating Union soldiers, they discovered thousands of rifles and cartridge boxes as well as hundreds of straggling comrades too weak to keep up with the fleeing Union troops. Still Forrest pursued. By the end of June 11, 1864, Sturgis' army was without food and ammunition, and the infantry had begun abandoning their shoes; their feet too blistered and bloody to cover them.

The Battle of Brice's Cross Roads cost the Union forces over a quarter of their strength, with Forrest inflicting nearly 5 times as many casualties as he suffered. Additionally, all the Union's artillery, ambulances, wagons, ammunition, camp equipment, 184 horses and mules, and over 2,000 rifles were now in the hands of Confederate forces, all due to Forrest's brilliant strategy and relentless pursuit. This extraordinary victory demonstrated not only what inferior numbers could accomplish under the right command, it showed what Forrest himself was capable of achieving.

---

[40]   Brown, Dee. (Stan Banash, editor). *Dee Brown's Civil War Anthology*. Page 203.

The Battle of Tupelo

While the Atlanta Campaign was still in full swing, Forrest was involved in a clash at the Battle of Tupelo from July 14-15. Once again, it was brought about by Union forces intent on pinning down Forrest and keeping him at a safe distance from Sherman's lines. Having already obliterated one Union army at Brice's Cross Roads, Sherman feared Forrest might move into Tennessee and damage Union supply lines that were already going to be extended as his army pushed its way into Georgia. Sherman ordered Union Major General A. J. Smith to march south from Memphis and "follow Forrest to the death, if it costs 10,000 lives and breaks the Treasury."[41]

After maneuvering for several days, General Smith found himself confronted at Tupelo by Forrest and his commanding officer, Major General Stephen D. Lee. Fully aware of the inherent danger of fighting the crafty Forrest on the open battlefield, Smith ordered his men to dig in and wait for the Confederates to come to them. Left with no alternative but assault the fortified Union positions, Forrest and Lee unleashed a series of vicious attacks against the Union lines, but they were made in unsupported, piecemeal fashion. The attacks seemed uncharacteristically ill-conceived for the usually methodical Forrest, who would later assert that the Union's defenses were unassailable.

Handily resisting Forrest's haphazard attacks, Smith managed to turn the tables on Forrest and deliver the first significant beating Forrest suffered. After two days of fighting, Forrest's troopers had been defeated, and Forrest was wounded in the foot in the process. Smith eventually withdrew his forces to Memphis, convinced that Forrest's men wouldn't be taken, much to the chagrin of Union leaders who hoped to permanently sideline him.

Although Smith had not succeeded in stopping Forrest to the extent Sherman had hoped for, he had delivered Forrest a staggering blow and severely damaged his ability to impede Sherman's campaign. Historians acknowledge that the Battle of Tupelo (and Forrest's defeat) significantly contributed to Sherman's ability to seize Atlanta and the momentum his army picked up there after.

The End of the War

Throughout the summer and fall of 1864, Forrest led numerous raids, including a well-documented one straight into the heart of downtown Memphis in August 1864 while it was occupied by Union forces. He also raided a Union supply depot at Johnsonville, Tennessee, on October 3, 1864 (the Battle of Johnsonville), which caused millions of dollars in damage.

---

[41]   National Park Service website.

However, the Confederacy was in its death throes. When General Joseph Johnston retreated to within 3 miles of Atlanta, President Jefferson Davis replaced him with John Bell Hood, an aggressive general who had served effectively as a division commander at places like Gettysburg and Chickamauga but was now being promoted a station too high. Hood lost Atlanta after a series of attacks on Sherman's larger army before heading north, hoping to bring the fighting back into Tennessee.

In early December, Forrest's men fought along with Hood's Army of Tennessee in the Confederacy's most decisive, and disastrous, campaign. At the end of 1864, Hood effectively destroyed his army in a series of vicious but futile frontal assaults against General George H. Thomas's well-entrenched Army of the Tennessee. At the Battle of Franklin, Hood managed to lose over a dozen field generals, including half a dozen killed, among them Patrick Cleburne, the "Stonewall of the West". Weeks later, Hood was routed in similar fashion at the Battle of Nashville. At the Battle of Franklin, Hood detached Forrest with a command in a diversionary method, hoping to draw Thomas's army out of its entrenchments. The ruse failed, but Hood attacked anyway, despite having less men when they left with Forrest. Once again, Forrest chafed under what he viewed as incompetent leadership, arguing with Hood that he should be allowed to use his force to cut off a potential escape route in the case of victory. When Hood refused Forrest's advice, Forrest did so anyway.

On December 5, 1864, Forrest then engaged Union forces near Murfreesboro (where his army was effectively repelled at what would be known as the Third Battle of Murfreesboro), and on December 25, a portion of his army was taken totally by surprise and captured in their camp at Verona, Mississippi during a raid of the Mobile & Ohio Railroad by a division of Union Brig. General Benjamin Grierson.

Despite those setbacks, Forrest distinguished himself once again while covering the rear of the retreating Army of Tennessee after Franklin, earning him further recognition. In February 1865, Forrest was promoted to Lieutenant General and given the duty of guarding the frontier from Decatur, Alabama to the Mississippi River, where he continued his bold, relentless raids. With worn-out horses and dwindling manpower, he attempted to cut off an advance of three divisions led by Union Maj. General James H. Wilson south of Tennessee near Selma, Alabama, one of the South's last remaining centers of war-supply manufacturing. Although he was initially able to resist the Union advance, on April 2, his weakened troops were eventually forced to retreat, leaving Selma to the Union army.

Forrest continued to fight on until hearing news of Lee's surrender of his Army of Northern Virginia at Appomattox, which took place on April 9, 1865. Appomattox is widely remembered today as the end of the Civil War, but there still remained several Confederate armies across the country, mostly under the command of General Joseph E. Johnston. On April 26, Johnston surrendered all of his forces to General Sherman, and over the next month, the remaining Confederate forces would surrender or quit. The last skirmish between the two sides took place May 12-13, ending ironically with a Confederate victory at the Battle of Palmito Ranch in Texas. Two days earlier, Jefferson Davis had been captured in Georgia.

Forest maintained limited field operations until May 9, when he finally decided to quit the war. He had suffered several war wounds, and was legendarily credited with killing 31 Union soldiers and having 30 horses shot out from under him. Forrest is said to have quipped, "I was a horse ahead at the end,"

Whether that is true, what is certain is that Forrest gave a rousing farewell address to his soldiers before quitting the war:

"Civil war, such as you have just passed through naturally engenders feelings of animosity, hatred, and revenge. It is our duty to divest ourselves of all such feelings; and as far as it is in our power to do so, to cultivate friendly feelings towards those with whom we have so long contended, and heretofore so widely, but honestly, differed. Neighborhood feuds, personal animosities, and private differences should be blotted out; and, when you return home, a manly, straightforward course of conduct will secure the respect of your enemies. Whatever your responsibilities may be to Government, to society, or to individuals meet them like men.

The attempt made to establish a separate and independent Confederation has failed; but the consciousness of having done your duty faithfully, and to the end, will, in some measure, repay for the hardships you have undergone. In bidding you farewell, rest assured that you carry with you my best wishes for your future welfare and happiness. Without, in any way, referring to the merits of the Cause in which we have been engaged, your courage and determination, as exhibited on many hard-fought fields, has elicited the respect and admiration of friend and foe. And I now cheerfully and gratefully acknowledge my indebtedness to the officers and men of my command whose zeal, fidelity and unflinching bravery have been the great source of my past success in arms.

I have never, on the field of battle, sent you where I was unwilling to go myself; nor would I now advise you to a course which I felt myself unwilling to pursue. You have been good soldiers, you can be good citizens. Obey the laws, preserve your honor, and the Government to which you have surrendered can afford to be, and will be, magnanimous."

Chapter 5: The Postwar Years, 1865-1877

Forrest after the Civil War

Forrest may have given one of the most magnanimous farewell addresses of the Civil War, which is ironic on several levels. After all, literally nobody had fought harder than Forrest for the cause, which he was personally and financially heavily invested in, and the volatile Forrest had a legendary stubbornness and tenacity. Furthermore, in the decade after the Civil War, "Fort Pillow Forrest", as he was known in the North, would become the most notorious unreconstructed rebel and one of the most controversial men in America.

Founder of the Ku Klux Klan?

When Forrest finally gave up the fight and returned to Memphis, he found that his plantation had been leveled, his slaves freed, and his vast fortune confiscated. Financially wiped out, he resumed planting and sometime later became the president of the Selma, Marion & Memphis Railroad, which he helped promote. Forrest also became active in Democratic Party politics.

However, all of Forrest's postwar activity pale in comparison to his reputed involvement with another organization. Near the end of the 1860s, Forrest also reportedly became instrumental in the organization of what would become the Ku Klux Klan, and according to some accounts, may have been its first Grand Dragon. In fact, although no source has ever completely substantiated the rumors, Forrest has become widely recognized as the founder of the Ku Klux Klan, and whether the rumors are true or not, the rumors themselves have played a principal role in the shaping of Forrest's image, starting with the Klan's inception. Forrest never openly admitted nor denied the extent of his involvement, but reports state that while Forrest was a K.K.K. founder (and even took part in lynching), he also sought to have it disband in 1869 (both of which may be true).

As the Klan became a growing source of frustration for the North, Forrest was called before a Congressional Committee to give testimony about the Klan. While refusing to admit that the Klan existed, Forrest nonetheless justified subversive actions by vigilante groups, arguing that they were defending against Northern Republican aggression. When asked about the size of the Klan, Forrest estimated that the number of vigilantes was in the hundreds of thousands, although he "could not speak of anything personally" and got all his "information from others." Forrest was clearly refusing to directly answer the questions, but it was true that the Klan, even by the early 1870s, was not centrally controlled or even completely identifiable. If the Klan connections attributed to Forrest did exist, Forrest was now powerless to control or stop the terrorism being attributed to the Klan

Change of Heart?

During the last two years of his life, it seems quite likely that Nathan Forrest experienced what can best be termed a "change of heart," perhaps attributable to his wife Mary Ann. Although history would ultimately not credit him with much more than an indomitable, even ruthless method of warfare that proved remarkably effective, in his mid-50s, documents indicate that he not only ordered the dissolution of the Ku Klux Klan branch he headed, but went on to repeatedly disavow the race hatred it promoted, railed against racial discrimination, and even publicly appealed for social and political advancement for Blacks.

In Memoriam

Throughout the mid-1870s, Forrest's health began to fail him, brought about in part due to the many serious wounds he had suffered during the Civil War. Travelling to different parts of the country failed to help him, and Forrest died in Memphis, Tennessee on October 29, 1877 at the age of 56, probably of diabetes. Papers in the North were extremely critical of Forrest in obituaries. The *Boston Globe* sardonically referred to Forrest as "General Napoleon Bonaparte Forrest." The New York Times, while lauding "dignified" and "gallant soldiers" like Lee, criticized "Fort Pillow Forrest" for his "ruffianism" and "cut-throat daring." Meanwhile, those same qualities were being celebrated by Southerners. The *Memphis Daily Appeal* exhorted Forrest for "the courage of his heart, the valor of his principles, and the energy of his character," comparing his tactics to "the methods of the Crusaders." The *Charleston News and Courier* simply labeled Forrest the "hero of Tennessee."

Nathan Bedford Forrest's fighting tradition was also passed down in the family. Forrest's great-grandson, Nathan Bedford Forrest III (April 7, 1905--June 13, 1943) was a brigadier general in the United States Army Air Forces who died in service to his country, the first American general to be killed in battle in Europe.

Chapter 6: Forrest's Legacy

Though he remains as controversial as ever, Forrest is particularly honored in his home state of Tennessee, where his birth date, July 13, is officially observed and 32 historical markers have been placed, more than Illinois has for Lincoln. He is interred in a city park in Memphis bearing his name, which also features a large equestrian statue honoring him.

Although many Americans still have mixed feelings about Forrest and his accomplishments, historians have long considered him the most magnificent cavalry officer America has ever produced. During World War I, American newspaper accounts often referred to Forrest and his tactics glowingly, and Forrest's use of quick-hitting, fast moving mobile forces was considered a predecessor of the Nazis' blitzkrieg warfare. In the 1940s, Forrest was compared to Hitler for the first time, and it was a favorable one. The *Memphis Commercial Appeal* observed, "Hitler, more than anyone else, is applying Forrest's methods", and it was rumored Nazi generals had studied Forrest's tactics, leading Lawrence Wells to write a fictional tale about the Desert Fox, Erwin Rommel, traveling to America to study Civil War battlefields in *Rommel and the Rebel*.

Starting from Scratch

Although Nathan Bedford Forrest had virtually no formal education and no military training to speak of, he advanced from private to lieutenant general at an unprecedented rate - the first and only man to do so - during the Civil War, and he earned a reputation as one of the finest cavalry leaders ever in the field. Perhaps more than any other general in the Civil War, he instilled fear in his enemies, drew anger from his superiors, and garnered as much respect from his men as any officer of the war on either side of the conflict.

As his record demonstrated time and again, Forrest's personal bravery and capacity for fighting were nearly matched by his abilities as a battlefield tactician. Wounded no fewer than four times, records show that he also had at least twenty-nine horses shot out from under him or wounded beneath him. And while many in authority initially thought that an uneducated, untrained soldier who hadn't attended West Point would never be effective, let alone attain greatness, his personal toughness and dedication were never in question, and always amply evident. His often-repeated motto regarding battle was: "I always make it a rule to get there first with the most men. War means fighting, and fighting means killing. Get them scared and keep the scare on them."[42]

---

[42]   Lanning, Michael. *The Civil War 100*. Pages 84--85.

He despised cowardice, remained fully committed to the cause even after everyone else had abandoned it, and had no tolerance for incompetent leadership. This is well exemplified by his reaction to General Braxton Braggs' refusal to pursue the Union Army at Chickamauga, He punctuated his stance by taking his cavalry to Texas without official authorization, never fighting under Bragg again. And while many would see this as a blatant act of insubordination, Forrest clearly saw himself as loyal to a *cause*--not the whims of those who prove ineffectual at championing that cause.

For all the reasons Northern commanders found Forrest an incessant thorn in their sides and Southern commanders found him a difficult man to swallow, and even harder to command. It is a testament to how effective Forrest was that a man who gave several commanding officers major headaches was eventually promoted to the highest rank the Confederacy had to offer.

On the Subject of Mexico

Unlike most of the principle leaders of the Civil War who received the country's best military training at West Point and "cut their military teeth" on the Mexican-American War, Forrest never aspired to a career in the military and thought it hardly worthwhile to squabble with Mexico over land. Indeed, his momentary foray into military life in 1841 was precipitated on the idea that Mexico may not stop at Texas but invade the United States.

He did, however (at least momentarily), consider conquering Mexico himself, and told friends he could do so in six months with 30,000 men and 20,000 rifles. Ever the businessman, he said he would then confiscate the country's mines and considerable Church assets, set himself up as ruler, and then open up the country to the two hundred thousand Southerners he expected to flock there. Forrest was always a man of big ideas, but he didn't engage in idle bragging either. Had the Civil War not interrupted his ambitions, and had he lived longer, who knows what he may have accomplished. He had already gone from broke to being extravagantly wealthy by the time he reached 40.

On Education

Forrest's lack of formal education is well reflected in his writing (once likened to that of a child for whom English was his second language) as this correspondence to onetime business associate Minor Meriwether demonstrates: "All diferances [sic] between us air satisfactory setled [sic] and I asure [sic] you that thair [sic] is no unkind feling [sic] towards you from me. I have . . . never felt unkindly to wards your Self only when I felt you was using your influence [sic] against my Intrest [sic]."[43] Even so, Forrest is said to have developed an emphatic knack for oral sentence structure, which effectively served to counterbalance his illiteracy. Thus despite his lack of proper schooling, he clearly understood the need to communicate explicitly, and taught himself to do so.

His farewell address to his troops makes clear that, even if he had help writing and articulating his ideas, he was capable of stirring thoughts.

Sensibilities

While Forrest's detractors found much to fault in his personality, those who knew him best describe a man whose virtues outweighed his vices. Perhaps it should be expected of a rough and tumble man of the frontier that he often spoke profanities and had an admitted fondness for gambling, including reportedly gambling very large sums of money when he was wealthy. At the same time, Forrest had some "Southern Gentleman" attributes to his personality as well, exhibiting perfect manners for women and clergy. Forrest never drank or used tobacco, and he openly showed delight in the presence of children.

He was known for his love of horses and known to race on more than one occasion, despite suffering chronic boils. And despite his lack of education, he was witty, often with a knack for humor. At a dinner party held during the Civil War, a woman of high social status Forrest why his hair had turned gray while his beard remained dark, to which he replied, "Because I tend to work my brain more than my jaws!"

Forrest was clearly graying during the Civil War

---

43   Hurst, Jack. *Nathan Bedford Forest, A Biography.* Page 8.

Race Relations

Forrest's legacy will almost certainly be marred permanently by Fort Pillow, his slave trading, and his well documented disdain of African Americans. Even in his own day, he was one of the most hated men in America, and everything evil that could be alleged about Forrest eventually was.

For example, one oft cited but almost certainly apocryphal story involves an incident reported by Union private William J. Mays, who claims to have witnessed Forrest approach two Negro women with their three children and say, "Yes, damn you. You thought you were free, did you?" as he shot them all dead.[44] Then of course, there were the alleged atrocities against black soldiers at Fort Pillow. Of the alleged massacre, a story in *Harper's* stated, "The annals of savage warfare nowhere record a more inhuman, fiendish butchery than this, perpetuated by the representatives of the 'superior civilization' of the States in rebellion."[45]

Although much has been made of Forrest's questionable conduct at Fort Pillow, some historians have argued Forrest had a genuine sense of humanity concerning his slaves, one that became more prominent with age. Of course, that does not seem to square with what Forrest did or wrote, leaving some biographers to suggest it may have been as much a matter of good business as humane treatment.

In the field, as well as on his own plantation, Forrest had a reputation for not separating members of black families, and made it a habit of providing hygienic care and clean clothes to his slaves. He even offered 45 of his own slaves their freedom if they would agree to serve as teamsters to his Confederate troops, which they did and were rewarded as promised. And as several newspaper accounts note, there were hundreds of African Americans among the thousands of Whites at Forrest's funeral, indicative, perhaps, of an understanding they possessed about the enigmatic Forrest that many others did not.

Forrest frequently argued the hypocrisy of those who professed to be outraged by slavery's inhumanity, particularly what he viewed as jealousy of the economic advantage slavery afforded slaveholders. He noted that while there was considerable favor by Northerners to grant the land of Southern slave owners to their former slaves after the Civil War, there was no interest whatsoever in providing freed slaves Northern land and protecting their civil rights and safety by bringing them North. Forrest asserted that few Northern states even permitted Blacks. Thus, Forrest was quick to lend his respect for Southerners who stood by their beliefs (regardless of what those beliefs entailed) and were willing to fight for them, but withhold it from those Northerners who engaged in war without honor or conviction of purpose.

---

[44] Wright, Mike. *What They Didn't Teach You About the Civil War.* Page 220
[45] Gallagher, Gary W. *The Union War.* Page 98.

Forrest in Profile

Biographers describe Forrest as standing 6'2 and weighing 210 pounds, a powerful and dominant build. At the same time, Forrest was described as remarkably agile, with steady, piercing eyes. No matter what anyone thought of the man, there was no doubt that he possessed a commanding presence.

Of course, Forrest is also described as a violent, passionate man who struggled with emotions his entire life and for whom discipline and order were essential to his stability. Naturally intimidating, he used his skills as a hard rider and fierce swordsman to great effect, both on and off the field, and was even rumored to sharpen both the top and bottom edges of his saber and wield it with particular zeal.

In his popular novel about the Battle of Shiloh, Shelby Foote, in covering the battle, wrote Forrest's sword "looked ten feet long." Foote probably wouldn't have gotten much of an argument out of the Union soldiers who had the misfortune of fighting him.

Selected Bibliography

Bearss, Edwin C. (William C. Davis and Julie Hoffman, editors). "Joseph Wheeler," In *The Confederate General*, Vol. 6. Harrisburg, PA: National Historical Society, 1991.

Brown, Dee. (Stan Banash, editor). *Dee Brown's Civil War Anthology*. Santa Fe: Clear Light Publishers, 1998.

Burns, Ken (PBS director). *The Civil War, Episode 7,* "Most Hallowed Ground" PBS Home Video. Accessed via Hulu, 4.26.2012.

Gaffney, P. and D. Gaffney. *The Civil War: Exploring History One Week at a Time*. New York: Hyperion, 2011.

Gallagher, Gary W. *The Union War*. Cambridge: Harvard University Press, 2011.

Gott, Kendall D. *Where the South Lost the War: An Analysis of the Fort Henry—Fort Donelson Campaign, February 1862*. Mechanicsburg, PA: Stackpole Books, 2003.

Hurst, Jack. *Nathan Bedford Forest, A Biography*. New York: Vintage Books, 1994.

Lanning, Michael. *The Civil War 100*. Illinois: Sourcebooks, Inc., 2006.

National Park Service website: http://www.nps.gov/tupe/why-the-battle-happened.htm. Accessed 4.28.2012.

Phillips, David. *Civil War Chronicles: Crucial Land Battles*. New York: Metro Books, 1996.

Sherman, W. T. (Charles Royster, notes). *Memoirs of General William T. Sherman*, Vol. I and II. The Library of America, 1990.

Wright, Mike. *What They Didn't Teach You About the Civil War*. Novato, CA: Presidio Press, 1998.

Printed in Great Britain
by Amazon

29973595R00057